Surviving a Stroke

Recovering and adjusting to living with hypertension

Mike Ripley

Editors Richard Craze, Roni Jay

LARGE PRINT
Oxford

First published in Great Britain 2006
by
White Ladder Press Ltd.

Published in Large Print 2007 by ISIS Publishing Ltd.,
7 Centremead, Osney Mead, Oxford OX2 0ES
by arrangement with
White Ladder Press Ltd.

British Library Cataloguing in Publication Data
Ripley, Mike
    Surviving a stroke: recovering and adjusting to living
    with hypertension. – Large print ed.
    1. Ripley, Mike
    2. Cerebrovascular disease – Patients – Great Britain
    – Biography
    3. Cerebrovascular disease – Patients – Rehabilitation
    – Popular works
    4. Large type books
    I. Title
    616.8'1'0092

ISBN 978–0–7531–5671–1 (hb)
ISBN 978–0–7531–5672–8 (pb)

Printed and bound in Great Britain by
T. J. International Ltd., Padstow, Cornwall

BURY
METRO

Please return/renew this item
by the last date shown.
Books may also be renewed by
phone or the Internet.

www.bury.gov.uk/libraries

Dedication

This book is dedicated to my wife Alyson, our children — Beth, Felicity and Guy, who were 15, 11 and eight at the time — and to my long suffering GP Dr David Milne. All of them are still managing to put up with me.

Somehow.

Contents

Contents

Information panels

Introduction

In January 2003, at the age of 50, I had a stroke. I knew nothing about strokes, had no idea what my blood pressure was, or should have been, and had never spent a night in hospital.

Exactly a year later, to the very day spookily, a crime writing friend (herself a stroke victim when 44) sent me a copy of Robert McCrum's book *My Year Off* and suggested that I write a similar memoir.

I knew of Robert McCrum — indeed, I had met him once at a party in London and found him a very charming man — but I had never read his book until now. It is a tender and courageous story of how Robert, at the age of 42, suffered what he calls "an insult to the brain".

Unlike Robert McCrum, I did not keep a diary — I never have — but from the moment I entered hospital, I began to collect "material"; rehearsing scenes in my mind, filing them away, as novelists do, for future recycling.

Because I write comic crime thrillers, I have always looked for the farcical or humorous potential in a situation. It is not difficult to find humour within a National Health Hospital, even if at times the humour is slightly black. This may come across as cynical or perhaps even cruel, but it is not meant to. For me, humour was a way of averting hysteria during the most stressful and frightening experiences of my life. The nurses who treated me with great patience and gentleness had heard all the jokes before, but had the good grace to pretend they were not only fresh but funny.

Stroke is the cruellest of afflictions, a destroyer of lives in more ways than one. Ignorance of its causes and consequences are stroke's greatest allies. If this book dispels some of the myths and gives hope and comfort to survivors and those who care for them, then it will have served its purpose.

I would point out to readers that I was very, very lucky in what happened to me.

Thousands of others, each year, are not.

CHAPTER
ONE

A day that will live in infamy

Saturday 18th of January 2003 — the perfect time for a surprise attack.

That evening, my wife Alyson and I settled down to watch the DVD of *Pearl Harbor*, the only thing left worth renting in our local Blockbuster (it was a bad night on TV).

As it ended, I could remember a few of the special effects, but none of the dialogue and none of the actors and realised that I must have been asleep for large chunks of the movie. As I stood up to unload the DVD player, I promptly fell over and Alyson immediately asked how I had managed to get drunk without leaving the room for two hours.

"It must be that flu bug that's going around," I suggested lamely.

"Then why is your speech slurred?" she asked.

I was not aware that it was and said I was going to bed, and promptly walked into the door frame.

That was how it started.

The next morning I awake with no immediate memory of the problems of the night before.

And then I try to get out of bed.

It is as if I am in a spinning room on a boat in high seas, and I'd had a few drinks. My left arm tingles as well, as if I had slept on it and the arm and hand had "gone to sleep". I was not unduly worried about this as I had suffered similar instances of such "pins and needles" for years and had never taken it particularly seriously. Perhaps I should have done; perhaps they were the warning signs.

I am so unsteady on my feet I have to sit on the edge of the bed to get dressed.

Alyson remembers a quote from the late James Callaghan, the former Prime Minister, when asked if he had any advice for young politicians: "When you get to 70, always sit down before putting your socks on."

I remind myself that I'm still 20 years short of 70, though at that moment it doesn't feel like it.

Being a Sunday, we take it easy but decide that unless I feel much better in the morning, I will be going to see the doctor and not to work.

For the last three years I have been supplementing my meagre royalties from writing comedy crime novels with the equally meagre salary of a field archaeologist, digging mainly Romano-British sites in north Essex. Currently I am working on a dig in Colchester, our nearest town. Rescue archaeology on a building site in midwinter is not everyone's ideal, but this is a fascinating site just outside the west gate of the Roman capital of Britain and there's less than a month to go before the developers take over completely.

I had promised to write a proposal for an educational poster for schools, explaining what we had uncovered, over the weekend and email it to my boss. It was something which should have taken me no more than 15 minutes.

After two hours at the computer keyboard, I admit to myself that something quite serious is wrong. I am typing absolute garbage and hitting keys without realising it, my left hand seemingly out of control. Drenched in sweat and getting ever more angry with myself, I resort to one finger typing and eventually I complete a message of perhaps 200 words and press "Send". In total, that one email has taken me nearly six hours.

Alyson and I put a brave face on things over dinner, so as not to alarm the children, and I go to bed early, hitting every door frame with my left shoulder on the way.

The next morning, Monday, is a blur. Somehow the kids get to school and then Alyson drives me to our local doctor's surgery. She has telephoned to demand an immediate appointment in a voice which struck fear and awe into a medical receptionist — something I have never managed to do.

I am quickly shown in to see a female doctor whom I don't know and I introduce myself from the doorway of the consulting room by saying:

"Is it possible, doc, to have a stroke while you're asleep and not realise it?"

From across the room and without getting up from her chair, she says: "Yes it is. And from the way you're leaning, yes, you have."

What is a stroke?

Surprisingly few people actually know what a stroke is. There are popular misconceptions that a stroke has something to do with a heart attack and that they only happen to the elderly.

A stroke (often referred to as a **CVA** or **Cerebrovascular Accident** or **Attack**) happens when the blood supply to the brain is disrupted, most commonly when a blood clot blocks an artery or when a blood vessel bursts and bleeding occurs.

The term "brain attack" is being used more frequently, especially in America, where the George Washington University Hospital has a Brain Attack Team offering emergency treatment to stroke patients.

Strokes can happen to anyone and current medical thinking is that strokes among young children happen more than was ever previously imagined.

The doctor helps me to a chair and does a few simple tests involving my making fists and pushing them against the palms of her hands. She also wiggles two fingers from each hand at the sides of my head to see if my field of vision is affected. (This test, the wiggling fingers, is known as "making angry bunnies".) She also has lots of questions about when I think this could have happened and repeatedly asks if I have suffered any headaches, and I insist I have not.

6

I realise now (though at the time the questions just seemed irritating) that the doctor was trying to establish whether I had had a TIA — a Transient Ischaemic (eye-skee-mick) Attack, or "mini-stroke" — from which it can be possible to begin to recover after 24 hours.

Alyson agrees to drive me into our local hospital and the surgery doctor rings the Accident & Emergency department to warn them I am coming, so there will be no delay. We know she did this, because we heard her do it, but when we arrive less than 15 minutes later no one there has heard of me and our arrival is something of a surprise. My wife, however, can be quite insistent about things when she sets her mind to it and we soon have a nurse filling out paperwork and, again, asking how long I have felt like this and whether I have a headache or not. Once more I am insistent that I have not.

We are shown into the Accident & Emergency ward — by this time it is around 11 a.m. — and I am allocated a bed behind green screens and one of those sexless, backless hospital gowns. I say how quiet it all seems; not at all like the television counterparts of Casualty or ER but, as Alyson points out, it isn't a Saturday night just after the pubs have chucked out.

After a while, I have no idea how long, a young Indian doctor pulls back the screen curtain, looks at some notes and says: "Now then, what about these headaches?"

For the third time I plead that I don't have a headache, but am in danger of getting one if anybody else asks me that question.

The doctor repeats the tests done by my local GP, organises a blood sample and says I will be admitted to MAU — the Medical Assessment Unit — whatever that is. Then he smiles, politely says goodbye and withdraws behind the screens. I never see him again.

It seems that within seconds I am on the move as a porter arrives to push my trolley bed to this mysterious MAU. Now I am in the system things seem to be moving with impressive speed.

In fact my first ride on a hospital trolley lasts all of 20 seconds: out of A&E, around the corner and into a corridor where several other patients were double parked.

"Sorry, but we need the space in the ward," says the porter, "and you'll have missed lunch so I got you some sandwiches."

He places a plastic pack of sandwiches on my chest, puts the brakes on the bed wheels and leaves me there. I never see him again either.

In that corridor, Alyson and I agree that if I ever put this scene in a book or script, I will be accused of resorting to corny old clichés about the National Health Service. To be honest, lying there staring up at a blank white ceiling, it is actually quite tranquil and somewhere nearby there is a window open which makes the corridor several degrees cooler than the (to me) overheated A&E ward.

I tell Alyson not to stand about in the corridor but to go home, sort out the kids and come and find me later in this mysterious MAU — and to bring my shaving gear and, above all, a book to read. Or at least I think I say something like that, for I am drifting off to sleep and it simply seems too difficult to stay awake.

I was not to know that the four hours sleep I got in that corridor that afternoon was to be the longest uninterrupted period of sleep I was to have in over a week.

Who do strokes affect?

Just about anyone could have a stroke. Strokes are equal opportunity attackers.

There are thought to be about 100,000 first strokes a year in the UK and whilst usually associated with the elderly, 10,000 of those strokes affect people under 55, including children.

In the UK, USA and Australia, stroke is regarded as the third most common cause of death and a leading (if not *the* leading) cause of adult disability.

Particular groups at risk are thought to be: anyone with high blood pressure (**hypertension**) or where high blood pressure runs in the family, people who suffer from hardening of the arteries, angina, abnormal heartbeats or diabetes, those of Afro-Caribbean or South-Asian descent, those who are physically inactive and those who smoke. (Smoking is said to increase the risk of stroke *threefold*.)

Since 2004, most major regional hospitals in Britain have established dedicated Stroke Units, which (in theory) combine acute nursing care with rehabilitation techniques including: physiotherapy, occupational therapy and speech therapy.

When I feel the bed moving again, it is dark outside. I can tell that from the corridor windows as we roll along, but I have no idea of the time as it seems far too much of an effort to lift my left arm and look at my wristwatch. Similarly I cannot summon the energy to raise my head to see who is pushing me or where we were going.

I am delivered to the MAU, the Medical Assessment Unit (what Americans call "Triage"). This is a temporary ward, which is National Health shorthand for a space to put beds which is not a corridor. It is quite an airy space, with lots of glass windows which make me think of a large conservatory tacked on to a country house. There are perhaps six beds, arranged in a semi-circle facing a large desk unit which is the nurses' station, though there do not appear to be any nurses.

There must have been somebody on duty as I was transferred to the last bed in the semi-circle, conveniently close to the toilet, and there is no way I can manage that on my own. The bed seems to have at least a hundred pillows, each with a mind of its own, and it is like trying to get comfortable on a toboggan going down a scree slope. I realise that if I slip to the right, my left arm does not have the power to pull me back upright and it begins to dawn on me that the whole of my left side is not responding at all.

Suddenly, Alyson and our three children are at my bedside, armed with a sports bag containing washing and shaving things, pyjamas and the book I had specifically requested (though I did not remember): Gore Vidal's *The Golden Age*, which I had been trying to find the time to read for two years.[1]

I have no news to tell the family, as I had not been seen or talked to by anyone about my condition since that morning in A&E. No, wait, there is one piece of news, but I can't actually tell them *because I can't speak*. I can hear them; I can understand them; I can think of replies to their questions; but the words simply won't form in my mouth.

I am still trying to come to terms with this when a nurse appears and asks me what I ordered for dinner. This is the most difficult question in the world and I flounder for any sort of answer, unable to say anything, lying in bed at a ludicrous angle. *What did you order from the menu?* the nurse asks, and Alyson repeats the question. I have absolutely no recollection of ever seeing a menu, let alone choosing from one, but the nurse, relentless, presses on: *Has anyone shown you the menu?* She is pitiless in her interrogation and must have been in the Gestapo in a previous life. Pretty soon I am willing to tell her who my contacts in the Resistance are, where the secret radio is hidden and

---

[1] Two years on, telling this story, a neuro-psychologist expressed amazement that I had been conscious enough at this stage to ask not just for something to read, but a specific book.

what the code is, but all I can manage is a shake of my head.

Alyson takes over and orders me a cheese omelette, partly because it's the only thing left on the imaginary "menu" but mainly because she's quickly realised it will be the only thing I can manage to eat with one hand.

Even that is a bit of a trial. Being a "temporary", staging post ward, the MAU lacks some of the comforts of a normal ward. I couldn't care less about the lack of a television, but trying to eat one handed without any sort of tray on which to rest the plate is a farce. With Alyson's help, I slide out of bed on to the one chair we have been allocated and use the bed as a table. Even so, more food ends up on me than in me.

I experience an awful revelation, which comes to me in slow motion: *I am no longer able to use a knife and fork* and even more worrying, *I keep missing my mouth when I try to feed myself.* My dessert arrives — a pot of yoghurt, which Alyson has to open for me and even hold steady while I spoon it vaguely towards my face.

I feel a dark wave of depression flooding over me, the feeling that I am totally useless I am actually relieved when Alyson announces that it is time to get the kids home for dinner. Before she goes, though, she insists on helping me change into pyjamas, as my hospital smock is spattered with food particles, and heaving me back into bed. She keeps saying "Look at me" and staring into my face. Days later she tells me that the left side of my face had "slumped" and gone slack, though of course I cannot feel this and thankfully there are no mirrors in the MAU.

The family departs with a lot of very nervous smiles, hugs and kisses and I determine to do some reading just to reassure myself that my brain is still working even if my body is not.

Reading turns out to be as frustrating as eating or simply trying to stay in bed. Gore Vidal's *The Golden Age* is a superb book, part of his fictional history of the USA, but as a 467 page hardback, it's also bloody heavy for a one handed reader. The simple effort of holding the thing up and in focal length means that I gently slide down and to my right. I am on the edge of the bed, in serious danger of falling on to the floor, when I give up. I have at least been able to recognise words on the page even though I cannot concentrate long enough to make sense of them.

I cannot sleep and so I lie there and take stock of my surroundings. There are three or four nurses at the central desk/work station, all doing paperwork (something, I am soon to learn, which takes up an increasing proportion of their working day) and chatting about the availability of good rented accommodation in Colchester. To my immediate right the bed has been filled by a middle-aged man who is suffering from either an appalling skin disease or severe burns. He has a single sheet pulled up to his chin and he keeps as still as possible. We make eye contact, but he doesn't want to speak and I cannot.

On the other side of the ward, two other beds have sleeping patients I hadn't really noticed before and sitting on a third is a tiny old lady who has a procession of visitors, some civilians — family perhaps — and several nurses. She is referred to as Connie and although they keep their voices down to a whisper, it is clear that all the visitors are working to one end, which is persuading Connie that she really must get into bed and spend the night here. Connie is not objecting violently or anything, she just doesn't believe them and she puts her side of the argument quite forcefully. When nurses and relatives insist that she must get into bed, she suddenly stops complaining, jumps to her feet and begins to take all her clothes off.

Screens are hastily drawn around the bed and when they are pulled back, Connie is in the bed, staring rigidly at the ceiling. She doesn't say a word as the relatives (if that is what they are) depart and the nurses disappear down the corridor.

The MAU falls silent and the nurses' station is now deserted. The night shift operates from another station down the corridor, from where they can cover more than one ward. Of course I don't know this and it seems as if we patients have been deserted, although we all have a bell-push "panic button" alarm.

But we are not forgotten; we have a visitor, who studiously avoids the bed in which Connie is now sitting bolt upright (I should have noticed that warning sign) and makes a beeline for me, as the only patient obviously awake.

It turns out to be one of the hospital chaplains, a small woman in her sixties, with a weatherbeaten face, round rimless glasses and an aura of taking no nonsense. She is wearing a dog collar over a polo-necked shirt, a suede waistcoat and what look like jodhpurs. She carries a small leather-bound Bible like a cosh and she sits down on the one chair near my bed.

I am now regretting that when I arrived at the hospital that morning and one of the questions on my paperwork had been "Religious faith?" I had answered "None, I'm Church of England" because it seemed like a good joke at a time when I needed to be cheerful.

"Just arrived?" she asks and I think I had better answer before she goes for my kidneys with that Bible.

"Nnnnngggrrress," I say, or something like that. I think I am beginning to drool.

"And what do you do for a living?" she asks, peering over her glasses at me.

An innocent enough question, but I know there is absolutely no way I am going to be able to say the word "archaeologist" and so I concentrate my efforts to tell her about my "other job" as a writer.

I take a deep breath and say: "I write detective novels" though I have no idea what it comes out as.

"Of course you do," said chaplain, slapping the palm of her hand with the Bible as she gets to her feet and walks away.

Learn to recognise a stroke, because time lost is brain lost

Stroke is a medical emergency. Know these warning signs of stroke and teach them to others. Every second counts.

- Sudden numbness or weakness of the face, arm or leg, especially on one side of the body

15

- Sudden confusion, trouble speaking or understanding
- Sudden trouble seeing in one or both eyes
- Sudden trouble walking, dizziness, loss of balance or coordination
- Sudden, severe headache with no known cause

SOURCE: American Stroke Association

I try to sleep in the faint hope that I will awake to find this has all been a terrible dream but it is too hot in the MAU for me. I struggle to get out from under my sheets and blankets but they grip me like an anaconda.

I realise, to my horror, that I can feel nothing much at all down my left side now. As I lie there it is almost as if I can see my condition deteriorating by the minute. When I arrived in MAU just a few hours before I knew my left arm and left leg were not working properly, but now they don't seem to be working *at all*. I am also convinced that I will never speak out loud again.

Now I am seriously depressed and obsessed with the idea that the kids *must not see me like this*. If I could only get to a phone, I could ring Alyson and tell her not to bring them to see me tomorrow. I think even then I knew that was a ridiculous idea. For a start, I can't get out of the bed, let alone across the ward to the phone on the nurses' desk. There is also the slight problem of not being able to speak.

I try to accept the fact that I am a prisoner in my hospital bed. The elderly and seemingly frail Connie, however, does not accept that she is in hers.

I do not actually see her get out of bed. In fact I only become aware that she is missing from the ward when I hear a muffled commotion in the corridor and the slap-slap of a nurse's shoes. Faintly, I hear indistinct voices and then one loud and clear "I want a wee!". I suspect this is Connie rather than the nurse.

A door slams and after a while opens and there is the sound of a distant flushing of a toilet and then the footsteps start up again and Connie appears, escorted by a nurse who leads her to her bed and tucks her in, turning off the bedside light as she leaves. I am still hearing the nurse's footsteps echoing down the corridor as Connie slithers out of bed again and this time heads across the ward towards the toilet the other side of my bed.

"I need a wee!" she announces proudly as she sails by my bed. I am not sure how to respond. I don't think I can respond. All I can do is avert my gaze as Connie proves that she wasn't bluffing and that she has literally adopted an open door policy on such matters.

Her nurse must have picked her up on radar, for she reappears to escort Connie back to her bed. To my unprofessional, and rather bemused, eye there is nothing physically wrong with Connie. She can certainly move faster than I can, probably faster than I could before the stroke, and I cannot think why she should be in hospital. The problem is, neither can she. I suspect she is not so much ill as confused, but doesn't know it, whereas I know I'm confused as well as ill.

Connie settles down and I lie there with the only light showing in the ward. This attracts our next visitor like a moth, though I only notice him when he is at the foot of my bed and he coughs politely.

"Could I possibly examine you?" he asks.

He is a young Chinese guy, smartly turned out in a white coat with a stethoscope round his neck.

"I need the practice, you see," he adds in explanation, pushing his photo ID badge towards me so I can focus on it. As he does so, I notice from his wristwatch that it is two minutes to midnight, which seems an odd time for doctors' rounds.

Then I read his badge and see that he is a registered medical student and that his name is Kenneth Ow.

This is too good to resist. Though I haven't the power of speech to share the joke with him, I immediately foresee lots of Carry On situations in the future, after he has qualified, when a raised voice from behind a screen shouts: "Hey! That hurts, Doctor . . . OW!!!"

I wave him forward, inviting him to do his worst and when he asks what I'm in for I want to say "How do I know? You're the doctor" but I can't manage it. I just grunt and try and indicate that my left side isn't working.

"Do you have high blood pressure?" he asks, concerned.

I try to shrug my shoulders, which doesn't really come off as only one of them is working and I have to try and indicate "I haven't a clue" with my eyes.

As the GP had done that morning, the future Dr Ow tests the strength in my arms and even does the "angry bunnies" thing with his fingers to check my vision and then he asks me:

"Did I do that correctly?"

I try to nod enthusiastically and this seems to please him.

After he leaves, a thick silence descends on the ward, disturbed only by the constant drone of snoring. I remember thinking that I'll never get to sleep with that level of background noise and as soon as I think that, I nod off.

But not for long. Pretty soon I am awake again, and so is Connie, and this time it's up close and personal because she is standing at the foot of my bed going through my sports bag of spare underwear and muttering to herself as if Harrods have delivered the wrong order.

I can't speak and I can't move. I am totally at the mercy of this 70 year old lady with long white hair flowing down to her hips, who stands no more than five feet tall in her pink nightie and probably weighs about 70 pounds wringing wet.

There has to be a crushing line of dialogue somewhere to go with this situation, a snappy one liner or a Groucho Marx put-down, but I'm damned if I can think of it, so I hit the panic button hanging by the bed.

After an eternity (probably about 10 seconds) a nurse appears by my side. Connie is now holding my bag upside down and shaking it.

The nurse, deadpan, says: "Is there anything wrong?" and when I point at Connie, all of three feet away, she does a classic double take and says "Oh", then leads her gently back across the ward, an arm around her waist.

"I've lost my glasses," Connie wails.

"They're on the chair by your bed," the nurse tells her.

"I had them earlier."

"I know, I took them off for you and put them in the case. There they are."

"That's not my bed."

"Yes it is."

"This isn't my house."

And so it goes on for a good 10 minutes until the nurse finally persuades her to get into the bed and tucks in the sheets.

I feel a pang of sympathy for Connie. It is almost as if I have grassed her up but, at the same time, I hope the nurse has tucked those sheets tightly.

Mini-strokes

"Stroke" is a very appropriate term because for most victims, the symptoms come on literally "at a stroke", right out of the blue.

Some people do get a warning, of sorts, in the form of a TIA, which NHS Direct defines as "a temporary period of disturbance of body function lasting for less than 24 hours". This is usually an indication that part of the brain is not getting enough blood.

TIAs are more commonly called **mini-strokes** and in many cases, symptoms disappear within an hour, but where once thought fairly harmless they should "no longer be considered a benign event but rather a critical harbinger of impending stroke." (American Academy of Family Physicians)

There are over 30,000 TIAs in Britain each year and it is estimated that one in five TIA victims could have a major stroke within a month, the greatest risk being within the first 72 hours. Some people have experienced two or three TIAs before a full blown stroke some stroke survivors may have had one in the past and not realised it.

CHAPTER
TWO

Burglars

Day 2 in the MAU begins early, at 5.40 a.m. I know this because I have just spotted where the ward clock is and I take great pride in this achievement.

Though it is still dark outside, there are more lights on in the ward though there are no signs of any nurses. Still, who needs them? The toilet/bathroom is only six feet away (though it seemed much closer when Connie was making eye contact while using the facilities a few hours before) and I can think of no reason why I shouldn't visit it.

With considerable effort I free myself from the bedclothes and swing my legs over the side of the bed until my feet touch the floor. The coast looks clear (Connie is asleep — I checked) and I launch myself into the void like a Friday night High Street drunk, across an expanse of empty floor which has now assumed savannah proportions. By putting all my weight on my right leg and using a kamikaze stumbling shuffle gait, I manage to smash into the left side of the door frame of the toilet. I knew I had put up my left hand to cushion the impact but nothing had happened.

22

This is frightening, as I have to do the return journey somehow, but once in the bathroom there are enough strategically placed grab rails to enable me to pull myself around with my right hand. I use the toilet and even manage a one handed wash and a long drink of water as the central heating in the ward has left me dehydrated. Perhaps fortunately, there is no mirror in there.

From the door of the bathroom it looks an awful long way back to my bed and I seriously think about calling for help, only I can't speak (and it never occurred to me that the red cord next to the light pull would have summoned a nurse) which is also scary.

Taking a deep breath, I stagger towards the bed, dragging my uncooperative left leg along behind me. I manage maybe three steps and think I'm doing fine when suddenly the entire ward starts to spin and I decide that if I throw myself the last few inches, I should make it. I don't. My chin hits the mattress but the rest of me doesn't and I land painfully on my knees.

For the next hour — and now that I've found the clock I can time myself — I attempt to scale the north face of my bed by throwing my one working arm (the right) across the mattress like a grappling hook, trying to get a grip which I can use to haul myself up. My legs are now like dead weights, dragging me down, not even useful as rudders, but I eventually get my head and chest on to the bed and begin to crawl, face down, up it. I'm not helped in any of this by the fact that the bed keeps moving, deliberately edging away from me every time I inch my way further on to it, nor by the fact that my pyjama trousers have come loose and have slid down my legs. This is turning into a true comedy moment, but there is no one, thankfully, to appreciate my performance.

Eventually I get all of me off the ground and on the bed, just in time to greet the morning tea trolley which arrives in the ward like a Panzer. The nurse driving it looks at the state of my bed in horror and immediately helps me off the bed I've spent so long trying to get on to, to the chair, so she can remake it to textbook perfection in a matter of seconds. I'm grateful for the consideration as she helps me back in and wedges the pillows to support me, but the distraction means she forgets to leave me any breakfast. Or perhaps I hadn't ordered anything from the menu.

The morning passes as a blur but I do remember a nurse coming to take my blood pressure, though it never occurs to me to ask her whether the reading is high or low, or what it actually means.

At some point a doctor enters the ward "on his rounds". This doctor has a slightly hunted look about him, but hunted by the pack of white coated students who trail behind him rather than by the patients. He stands in the middle of the ward and his acolytes form a semi-circle around him while he points at each bed in turn with his clipboard. As he never comes closer than twenty feet to my bed, I can't hear what he's saying but at one point they all look at me. I think about waving to them, but settle for a simpering grin. It has little effect on them and they leave the ward as suddenly as they had arrived.

24

I have a succession of visitors to my bedside. Most welcome of all is an old friend called Julie who actually works at the hospital as a radiographer. She asks me if I've seen a doctor and if I've had "a scan". I say "no" to both, without asking what a "scan" is or why she thinks I should need one.

Julie asks if there's anything I need and when I suggest a packet of cigarettes she says: "Are you being serious?" I have to admit I'm not, because if Alyson found them she'd probably break my fingers. "Mine too," says Julie, who has known Alyson for quite a while.

No sooner does Julie head off back to work than I have another visitor. This is a woman wearing a suit and a badge I can't read but who seems to know who I am. She also asks if I've seen a doctor or had a scan and tells me I will be moving into something called Birch Ward for "rehabilitation".

Even though I have not much idea of what is going on, this is the first person who has said anything to me about the consequences of having a stroke — or at least I *think* that is what she was talking about. I don't think she ever actually used the "s" word.

Then it's time for the daily interrogation as another nurse I've never seen before demands:

"What did you order for lunch?"

"Nothing so far," I say in my defence.

"Hasn't anyone shown you the menu?"

"No," I say apologetically.

"Then I'll see what's left."

I'm beginning to suspect there is something I'm missing here. Why are they keeping this mythical menu from me? I must ask a passing nurse.

Then it hits me that I actually *could* ask a passing nurse if I wanted to. I realise that I have talked to Julie, to the lady from Birch Ward and a nurse that morning and *they have all seemed to understand what I was saying.*

Maybe I'm getting better.

The symptoms of a stroke

No two strokes are the same. They happen to different people for different reasons and their effects are varied and can be short lived or permanently disabling.

A weakness or paralysis (known as **hemiplegia**) of one side of the body is a common effect. Because the right side of the brain controls the left side of the body (and vice versa), the weakness or paralysis occurs on the *opposite* side of the body to the side of the brain where the stroke occurred. Put simply, if the "brain attack" is right sided, it will be the left side of the body which is affected; whilst a stroke in the left side of the brain affects the right side of the body.

Speech and language difficulties are also fairly well recognised effects of stroke. Many victims experience problems with speaking and understanding the speech of others, and with writing and reading. Persistent problems with speech (known as **dysphasia**) are more common when the stroke has affected the left side of the brain, as the left half of the brain controls language.

As stroke attacks the brain, it obviously interferes with normal mental processes such as thinking, learning, concentration, memory, reasoning and planning ahead. These tend to be known as **cognitive problems** and can include problems with perception, affecting what you see (visual perception) or hear (auditory) or touch (tactile).

It is thought that over a third of stroke victims experience **swallowing problems**, when nerves and muscles are damaged by the stroke.

All stroke victims suffer from **fatigue** and **mood swings** and many survivors often experience what are known as "stroke moments" (or **emotional lability**) which is a tendency to burst into fits of either uncontrollable giggling or crying.

With all these potential effects it should not come as a surprise to learn that stroke survivors are prone to **depression, outbursts of anger, low self-esteem** and a **loss of confidence**.

I decide to spend the afternoon exploring my surroundings, for now I think I have my speech back, I assume everything is coming back.

Big mistake.

I swing my legs over the edge of the bed and attempt to put on the dressing gown Aly has brought me. My left arm simply will not go into the sleeve, so I stand up to have a better stab at it, and promptly overbalance, falling back on to the bed three times and missing it completely on my fourth swoon. Having hauled myself upright, I abandon the dressing gown. Noel Coward never had this trouble.

I manage a sort of limping shuffle across the MAU to the corridor down which nurses and tea trolleys have come and gone, but I've no idea what's down the other end. I never do find out as halfway down I have to lean against the wall for support. I am convinced that if I fall over here, I won't be able to get up again. The corridor is totally deserted and I've foolishly wandered miles away from my panic button bell push. I'm not sure I can even turn around and shuffle back to my bed, but then I take in the fact that only a few inches away is a red door on which is a sign saying BATHROOM.

I grab the door handle in order to steady myself so I can rearrange my feet, but to my horror the door starts to swing inwards, taking me with it. The door is not locked, but the bathroom isn't empty.

There is Connie, sitting quite regally, kicking her feet out in front of her.

"I needed a wee!" she shouts.

I can actually hear that this is true but am incapable of either apologising or congratulating her for now panic has robbed me of speech. Somehow, I pull the door shut, manage to turn round and with an impressive turn of speed I lurch back into the MAU ward to plunge, exhausted and drenched with sweat, on to my bed.

Alyson and the kids come visiting late in the afternoon. She demands to know what the doctors have said and I can't tell her much as the one doctor I have actually seen did not come close enough for me to talk to him. I can, however, report that I am being moved to "Birch

Ward" whatever that is. Has anyone mentioned having a "scan"? Well, they might have, I can't be sure, it's all been a bit hectic really.

She tells me my face looks much better and my speech is less slurred than 24 hours ago and I show her and the kids that I can stand up, albeit unsteadily. Alyson takes one look at me and begins to draw the screens so I can change into clean pyjamas. She also goes out of her way to remind me that she packed shampoo and shaving gear in my bag and surely there must be a shower around here somewhere.

I agree that I need a shave and could probably manage one handed. Alyson looks at me thoughtfully and says maybe I should wait until she has checked the insurance policies. I *think* she is joking.

Dinner is served suddenly and without warning. This time I'm not even asked if I have ordered anything from "the menu" which I am pretty sure by now does not exist.

Alyson makes a caustic comment about how the chicken and rice concoction comes automatically with two paper sachets of salt, which can't be good for me in my condition. Our eight year old son Guy is positively horrified at the sight of the greyish main course (but then he criticises Gary Rhodes for using too much sugar and butter) and suggests I ask for salads in future. I promise I will, but only if he brings in some of his own recipe salad dressing.

The first messages of sympathy have started to arrive at home and Alyson reads me emails and recounts phone calls, with some of my long standing crime writing friends first off the mark.

Minette Walters and her husband Alec have sent best wishes and the offer of a convalescent holiday in Dorset with them as soon as I get out of hospital. An old and distinguished friend, the book dealer George Harding, has rung from Wales offering to drive over immediately if there is anything he can do. (Knowing George, this would mean turning up with a couple of bottles of brandy, which is a tempting offer.) Colin Dexter, the creator of Inspector Morse, sends the message: "Tell Mike that if I was a praying man, I'd be praying for him. But I'm not, so I won't be." And from my mother-in-law: "Probably serves him right."

Clots and bleeds

Strokes fall into two main categories, depending on how the blood flow to the brain is interrupted.

The most common type of stroke is the **ischaemic** stroke which occurs when a blood clot (or thrombus) blocks an artery serving the brain, disrupting the blood supply even if only temporarily. The reduced blood flow causes brain cells to die from lack of oxygen.

An ischaemic stroke can often be the result of a long term build up of cholesterol and other debris in the arteries. Smoking is often cited as a contributory factor as it "furs up" the blood vessels, just as limescale furs up water pipes.

A blood clot could form in one of the main arteries leading to the brain (a **cerebral thrombosis**) or a clot could form elsewhere in the body and be carried in the bloodstream to the head (known as a **cerebral embolism**). A clot may also form in one of the small blood vessels deep within the brain (known as a **lacunar** stroke).

The second category of strokes involves bleeding rather than a blood clot obstructing an artery and are known as **haemorrhagic** (hem-or-rajik) strokes. This is where a blood vessel bursts, causing a haemorrhage or "bleed".

An **intracerebral haemorrhage** is where a blood vessel bursts within the brain, and a **subarachnoid haemorrhage** is where a bleed occurs in the space between the brain and the skull.

In simple terms, these types of stroke are known as **clots** and **bleeds**.

When the brain is deprived of its blood supply (and therefore its oxygen), this is called **infarction**, a word usually associated with heart attacks, and 85% of all strokes are due to infarction. The infarct can be tiny or could affect half the brain. The effect that an **infarct** has on a person, though, is not just how large it is, but where it is in the brain.

I am the only patient in the MAU to have visitors and when the family leave, the ward goes quiet, settling itself down for the night even though it's still not yet 6.30 p.m.

I decide to make a concentrated attack on the Gore Vidal novel, though it is so heavy I have to put a pillow under it for support, but by lying on my side I can get the pages into focus. I can see the words but they make absolutely no sense.

31

I am thankful for the distraction when another patient is wheeled in and transferred smoothly and swiftly into the bed next to the ominously quiet Connie. Our latest recruit is a man, but that is all I can tell from across the ward. He takes no interest in his new surroundings and settles down immediately to sleep.

The female chaplain appears, still in jodhpurs and waistcoat and does a quick circuit to suss out the new arrival, but he's not interested and she leaves quickly, ignoring me and giving Connie's bed a very wide berth.

I go back to Gore Vidal and find that I'm on Page 17, though I have absolutely no recollection of how I got there. Then I am distracted by Connie's attempts to engage her new neighbour in conversation. I can't make out all the words at first, but I can tell that Connie's affected upper class drawl betrays an underlying trace of native Essex. Not the Estuary English associated with Essex Girls, but the genuine east coast twang.

"I don't know why I'm in here," she is saying, "there's been a terrible mistake. I've no idea what all these other people are doing here. They shouldn't be here."

There is more on this tack; a lot more. At first the newcomer in the next bed grunts non-committally at her, then turns over, showing his back to her. Connie doesn't like this and ups the volume.

"I could telephone people, you know . . . . tell them to come and get me."

The new patient mutters something along the lines of: "I wish you bloody would."

32

"They shouldn't have left me here, you know. They were here, but now they've gone and I don't know where I am."

"Go to bloody sleep!" yells her neighbour.

Connie rises to the challenge; literally, by leaping out of bed. She is fully clothed and must have been lying under the bedclothes like that for hours.

In a flash she is standing at the side of the newcomer, poking him repeatedly in the shoulder with a stabbing finger, saying: "And you shouldn't be here either."

There is a distant buzzing noise and I realise that the man under attack has pressed his panic button, something which had never crossed my mind.

There are rapid footsteps and a nurse appears. The scene I am watching is like a very bad episode of *Miss Marple*, a little old lady with long white hair standing over an inert body, being restrained by a nurse.

"Now let's have you back in bed," says the nurse. "You're not even ready for bed! Where are your night things?"

"This isn't my bed!" shrieks Connie.

"Yes it is."

"No it isn't."

"It is for tonight."

"Why? Why should it be?"

I'm beginning to understand why there is no television on the MAU ward — it couldn't stand the competition.

The nurse starts to pull the screens around Connie's bed, whilst Connie gets into the spirit of things by taking off all her clothes.

"Now where are your night things, dear?"

"Don't you "dear" me. I don't even know why I'm here. I need a wee!"

"You're not going anywhere like that. Now where's your nightie?"

There is the sound of scuffling and then the screens rattle and shake and then open and Connie, hair flying, stomps across the ward, passing close to the foot of my bed, and into the toilet. Fortunately she has found her nightie, but still insists on an open door policy, so she can keep an eye on the nurse who is remaking her bed.

With the patience of a saint the nurse leads her back to her bed and tries to persuade her to get back in, which she does, but only after a twenty-minute argument about where Connie's glasses are.

"I haven't seen you wearing glasses," says the nurse.

"That's because they've gone, haven't they?" says Connie accusingly.

"They weren't on your bed. Could they be in your bag?"

"No they could NOT!"

Eventually the nurse finds Connie's glasses (in her bag) but tries to persuade her that she doesn't need them as it is time to go to sleep and hadn't she noticed that everyone else was asleep?

"He isn't," says Connie loudly, pointing a finger sternly in my direction. I try to melt into my pile of pillows and hide my face in my book.

There is a lull in the proceedings, almost a ceasefire. The nurse has tucked Connie in and left. The only light in the ward is my angle poise reading lamp.

I catch a glimpse of a white coat out of the corner of my eye. It is the nice Dr Ow on his nightly ramble looking for patients to practise on. He nods to me across the ward (does that count as being seen by a doctor?) but is really interested in the new arrival who has finally managed to get to sleep and is snoring loudly. Dr Ow shrugs his shoulders in resignation and tiptoes out of the ward.

As if on cue, several other patients start to snore and the decibel level rises considerably.

There is no way, I decide, that I am ever going to get to sleep with all this noise and as soon as I have that thought, I nod off.

It feels like I get 10 seconds of sleep, though in fact it is over two hours, and then I wake up. No, I don't wake up — I am woken up.

The bed is shaking and I am bouncing around on it. My first thought is that I am in the middle of an earthquake, then I realise the earth isn't moving, only I am.

It's Connie.

She is standing at the bottom of my bed and has grasped my right foot with both hands and is jerking it up and down. I have no idea whether she is trying to pull me out of bed, twist my foot off or just wake me up. Either way I can do little about it. I am flat on my back being toyed with by an unbalanced grandmother. I can't physically escape from her and I can't even beg for mercy as my throat has constricted and my voice has gone completely.

"Well now, this is a fine state of affairs, isn't it?" she says, yanking my foot up and down. "Just what do you and all your friends think you're doing in my house? I suppose you're burglars, aren't you? How would you like it if I phoned the police?"

Actually, I would like that very much, but I can't say so.

Connie continues to yank me up and down and I'm amazed by her strength. My book and several pillows have fallen on the floor and I'm in serious danger of being bounced out of the bed myself.

Clutching with my right hand at anything that might give me purchase, I grab my panic button, press it and keep it pressed.

As the long suffering nurse leads her back to her bed, Connie continues her rant about burglars, pointing to each fellow patient in turn saying: "There, there, and that one over there. What are they doing in my house?"

She is finally persuaded to get into bed and told she really *must* go to sleep now, but Connie doesn't really *have* to do anything. She's had burglars all right, burglars who have robbed her of her memory, just as a different burglar has taken away various parts of my body.

I am lying like a stranded whale, diagonally across my bed and the nurse has to come and straighten me out. She asks if there is anything I need and I make a major effort to get my voice working again.

"Sleeping pills," I manage to slur.

36

"Has the doctor prescribed sleeping pills for you?" she asks. "You can't have anything unless it's been prescribed."

"Not for me," I croak. "For her."

I point towards Connie's bed, which is now empty. The nurse heads for the corridor in pursuit.

I hear raised voices, the sound of a scuffle and then lots of footsteps and this time Connie is marched back into the ward by three nurses and a white coated figure who may well be a doctor, carrying a dish. I've seen enough movies to know there's a hypodermic in there.

Despite her protests, the screens are drawn around the bed and Connie is sedated.

The last thing I hear her say is:

"What are you doing? That's not a very nice thing to do to a person, is it? I mean, you wouldn't like somebody doing it to you, would you? It's just not being fair to a person, not fair at all."

And however much she has disturbed me, I have to admit she does have a point.

The cost of a stroke

Apart from being the third most common cause of death in England and Wales, after heart disease and cancer, stroke is the biggest single cause of severe disability with over 300,000 people affected at any one time. Stroke patients occupy around 20% of all acute hospital beds and 25% of long term beds. The cost of stroke to the National Health Service is estimated to be over £2.3 *billions* a year.

The *personal* cost of having a stroke is impossible to measure. A stroke can stop you working; can permanently disable you; can rob you of your livelihood, your sex life, the power of speech and the ability to think straight. A stroke isolates you from your brain and parts of your body, your family, your social life, your friends; the world as you knew it. Assuming, of course, it doesn't kill you.

CHAPTER
THREE

Birch Ward

Day 3 and I wake up still in the Medical Assessment Unit and it hasn't all been a dream. (It is only much later I learn that the hospital staff refer to the MAU as "The Twilight Zone".) It is about 8 a.m. and everyone seems to be awake and alert and I seem to have missed breakfast again.

The events of the night before suddenly come flooding back and I instinctively look over to Connie's bed and, with great relief, see that she is sleeping soundly.

I struggle to sit upright, floundering among my pile of pillows and a kindly nurse, seeing my pathetic efforts, comes to my aid. Even better, she's carrying a cup of what I assume is coffee. This is what I call top class service. The only trouble is she stops short of the bed, looks at a point somewhere above my head and says "Oh, I'm sorry" and begins to back away.

I can't work out what is going on and thrash around trying to see what she has seen. She takes pity on me and explains that there is a sign above my bed which says NIL BY MOUTH.

"You must be going for tests," she says, retreating.

"Tests? What tests? Nobody said anything about tests!"

At least that's what I'm *trying* to say, I'm not sure what it comes out as. All I can see is my cup of coffee disappearing the way all my phantom breakfasts have in the MAU. My distress communicates itself to the nurse, who, back at the central desk, makes several phone calls and gently prods at a computer keyboard. After about 10 minutes, she carefully carries the stone cold cup of coffee back across the ward and tells me that there has been a mistake. The Nil By Mouth sign wasn't meant for my bed at all. I'm going for a "scan", not "tests".

Immediately, I am more relaxed. I'm not sure what a "scan" is — or why I'm having one — but it sounds far less threatening than "tests" and, anyway, I've seen people having scans on TV. Plus, scans take place in Radiology, where our friend Julie works, so at least there will be a friendly face and someone to hold my hand.

In a strange way, I'm looking forward to the experience. It will, after all, be the first bit of actual treatment I've had, and I'm quite cheerful when a porter arrives mid-morning to help me into a wheelchair which he then propels at frightening speed along a maze of corridors to Radiology.

It is just my luck that it is Julie's day off, and I have to wait with a blanket around my legs for nearly an hour before a male nurse wheels me into the CAT Scan room and says cheerily: "You're not claustrophobic, are you?"

40

He tells me to lie on a sliding tray, rather like a bullet in the breech of a rifle, which goes into the scanner, a sort of large metal coffin affair. All I have to do is *keep still* and as the scanner feels more comfortable than my hospital bed, I almost fall asleep.

The experience is totally painless, not even really uncomfortable, and is over very quickly.

My porter is waiting for me and tells me that it's a quick trip back to the MAU to get my stuff and then it's off to Birch Ward and rehabilitation.

Many months later, an old friend and ex-Daily Mirror hack, George Thaw, tells me he had assumed I had made up the name of Birch Ward as it sounded like some sado-masochistic sex clinic. Boringly, it is named after the village of Birch, to the south-west of Colchester. At the time I was there, Birch Ward was in effect the hospital's Stroke Unit.

My departure from the MAU is like the getaway from a robbery in a charity shop. My porter tells me to "wrap up warm" as we'll be *going outside*, which sounds very exciting, so I have a blanket round my shoulders as well as one around my legs and my clothes, bag, shoes and Gore Vidal's *The Golden Age* are piled on to my lap.

"That's a big book," says the porter.

"And it's got a cracking page 17" is what I should have said, but I only think of that much later.

And then we're off and I haven't even got time to wave goodbye to Connie, who is fast asleep in bed — or at least that is what she'd like us to think.

We zoom down a long corridor with a mural on the wall which looks like something Picasso would have done in his Absinthe Years, and I vaguely recognise that this is one of the entrances to the hospital. The porter had not been kidding, we are going outside and a draught of icy cold fresh air confirms this.

As the automatic doors at the end of the corridor open, one particular scent comes in with the cold air. The doors open directly on to one of the hospital's service roads, but there is a sheltered area rather like a bus shelter, just before you reach the kerb. There are people huddled in this shelter — people in pyjamas, people in nurses' uniforms and just ordinary people — and that's where the smell is coming from.

We are passing the shelter in a blur before it registers with me that the smell, which seemed so familiar, is smoke. They are all having a crafty cigarette in that shelter and I've not had a smoke for three days. *Three days?* Surely one of them would let me have a quick drag . . .

But we're moving too fast, the porter pushing me across a road, heading for a glass and concrete tunnel and the ramp which leads to another part of the hospital site known as the Gainsborough Wing. For a few seconds we are totally exposed to the elements and I've been so distracted by the whiff of tobacco that I have failed to notice that it's snowing in the outside world!

This exposure to the elements lasts only a few seconds, for we are quickly in the shelter of the covered ramp and at the top of a rather steep incline is a lift which we take to the second, and top, floor. This is Birch Ward where, for the first time, I am to meet with other stroke patients.

What causes a stroke?

There is no single, simple answer to this question. There are, however, a number of contributing factors which are widely accepted to increase the risk of having a stroke:

- having diabetes
- high blood cholesterol
- being overweight
- excessive alcohol consumption
- eating too much salt
- heart disease
- high blood pressure (known as **hypertension**)
- lack of exercise
- kidney disease
- smoking

It is a misconception that sudden physical exertion, overwork, stress or bursts of anger cause strokes. In themselves, they do not, though they may well cause other problems.

I have a vague memory of stopping at a desk of some sort as my notes and charts (whatever they are) are handed over and then I'm escorted into "Bay D" and parked next to the first bed on the left.

Suddenly there are a lot of nurses, friendly ones, making me welcome and helping me settle into my allotted bed. I notice that they all have name badges and there's a Laura and a Lynn and a Louise. In fact, they all seem to begin with "L" but they are moving too fast for me to put faces to the name badges. One of them tells me in an excited whisper that there is a message for me to ring someone "At the BBC!"

Naturally, if it's the BBC, I have to answer immediately, even though I have no idea who from the BBC can be ringing me here, or why.

Louise, or Laura, or perhaps Lorna, helps me put on slippers and, putting my arm round her shoulder, she guides me to the reception desk to use the phone there, as the pay phone in the ward is — as is often the case — not working.

I am given a message slip on which someone has written the phone number for a reporter on Radio 5's *Brief Lives* programme and I immediately burst into a fit of giggles. I have to explain to the startled nurses that I am being asked to ring the weekly *obituary* show and when the reporter answers I cannot resist asking him if he knows something I don't.

The reporter naturally thinks I'm mad and explains that the thriller writer Gavin Lyall has just died and, as a critic and reviewer, would I be willing to pop into the studio in London and record an appreciation of his career. I tell him that I would be honoured to contribute to a programme about Gavin, but I'm rather tied up in a snowbound hospital, 75 miles away at the moment and I suggest he tries Harry Keating, the former *Times* reviewer. He's happy to take my suggestion, if only to get rid of me, as the poor guy probably can't understand my strangled attempts at conversational speech, which seem to get even more mangled when I'm using the telephone.

44

A nurse called Sarah, who wears a permanent and quite charming smile, asks me to get into bed so she can take my blood pressure. This involves an automatic machine wheeled up to my side, a cuff strapped to my right upper arm and a paper clip arrangement over one of my fingers to take my pulse. The machine goes beep and a jumble of figures flash up on the LCD screen.

I soon became used to the routine of the electronic blood pressure machine but on one occasion it obviously malfunctioned, emitting a high pitched whine and showing that I had a pulse of 888 even before it got around to my blood pressure. While the machine was taken away for recalibration, the nurses on duty all conferred about how to take my blood pressure "the old fashioned way" using a hand squeezed bulb and a stethoscope. None of them seemed to know how to do it without the automatic machine, apart from Sarah, who had done her initial training in the Philippines before coming to join the NHS.

It still doesn't occur to me to ask what the reading means or how important it is to my present condition. I have absolutely no inkling of how obsessed I am to become with those numbers.

High blood pressure

High blood pressure or **hypertension** is generally thought to be the most important risk factor for stroke, ischaemic heart disease and heart failure. People with high blood pressure are thought to be six times more likely to have a stroke than someone of the same age with normal blood pressure.

Blood pressure (usually written as **Bp**) increases naturally with age. It is typically low in the mornings and increases from afternoon to evening. It is also lower in the summer and higher in the winter. Because it varies so much, no single measurement in isolation is particularly useful. What is needed for a clearer picture is a series of readings over time.

After my stay in The Twilight Zone, the staff of Birch Ward seem to be going out of their way to make me welcome and I am repeatedly asked if there is anything I want, to which I reply: "A shower."

I am even brought one of the mythical menus, which really do exist, so I can order lunch and dinner from the choice of two dishes on offer. All the nurses are clearly embarrassed about the limits and inflexibility of the catering, which is sub-contracted out these days to save on NHS budgets. (Even though there is a pristine, fully equipped and totally unused kitchen on the ward as I later discover.)

One of the pretty young nurses — Lorna? — appears at my bedside and asks:

"Was it you who requested an assisted shower?"

"I haven't had an offer that good since 1976," I say, or at least that's what I try to say. Lorna smiles politely and I suspect she may have heard it before.

It is far from the erotic fantasy I had hoped for. Lorna (?) is the ultimate professional, staying the other side of the shower curtain, although she has to grab several times to prevent me from overbalancing. As she attempts to grab me in a bear hug through the wet, plastic curtain, the scene is more reminiscent of the Janet Leigh shower scene in *Psycho* than any cheap porno film I could have dreamed up.

The shower does revive me, though, even if I seem to go through about a hundred towels trying to dry myself. I persuade my shower buddy nurse that I can manage a one handed shave alone and I feel absolutely fine and ready for anything when I step out of the bathroom. And then I realise I haven't a clue where I am. I have managed to get lost less than 30 feet from my bed!

Fortunately a passing nurse takes pity on me and escorts me round a corner and into "D" Bay where all my things are arranged around Bed 1. I must remember that: Bed 1, D Bay, Birch Ward. That's my new address for the foreseeable future while I am in this mysterious place called "rehab".

Rehabilitation

Rehab involves relearning the skills and abilities lost as a result of the stroke; things you did automatically, without thinking, before.

The process can involve any number of professional health workers but, from my experience and what I have seen happen to others, rehab can only be successful with the full involvement and support of family and friends.

For many survivors, the first stage will involve **physiotherapy** whilst still in hospital. Using exercises and massage techniques to keep muscles and joints in working order, the aim is to help the survivor regain as much mobility as possible.

Occupational therapy is designed to help with the tasks of everyday life such as washing, dressing, eating, managing stairs and so on. An Occupational Therapist (OT) will probably encourage the resumption of old hobbies and leisure activities (or new ones) in order to relearn manual dexterity skills or improve memory and concentration.

Speech and Language Therapy (sometimes known as SALT units in hospitals) deals with communication problems after stroke. Many survivors have severe problems reading, writing and speaking and particular problems could include **dysarthia** (*diss-arth-ia*) being unable to form the sounds of speech, or **dysphasia** (*diss-faze-ia*), which means having problems understanding or using language. Speech Therapists may also be involved if a stroke survivor has problems with swallowing.

Clinical Neuropsychologists assess the mental effect of a stroke and the patient's mental abilities, sometimes referred to as **cognitive problems**.

The aim of rehab is to make the survivor as independent as possible. This is not a quick and easy process.

It begins in hospital and then possibly at a specialist rehabilitation unit, but it carries on in the home for many months, perhaps years, possibly for ever.

However mundane and ordinary to most people, virtually every simple task and every interaction with another human being is rehab for the stroke survivor.

D Bay has six beds. I'm in one corner and in the bed opposite is a wiry, dapper man of about 70, who is sitting up reading a paper-back. The man turns out to be Brian. I can't see what he's reading but I'm fascinated to find out if he's got beyond page 17 of whatever it is.

The middle bed opposite is empty, but obviously occupied, and the bed in the far corner contains the figure of a small, elderly man, bedclothes pulled up tight under his chin, revealing just his face, which is the colour of ash. This is John.

Next to me, in Bed 2, is Peter, who introduces himself in a thick Essex accent and insists on calling me "Mick" although no one has done that since my school days in Yorkshire.

Over the next week, Peter will go out of his way to show me the ropes of hospital life, rather like the long serving con forced to share a cell with a rookie inmate.

In truth, he looks terribly ill and is prone to sudden and very violent bouts of coughing and, as I discover in the middle of the night, much more. His skin looks as if it has been sandpapered and the slightest exertion leaves him breathless. He tells me he has been in hospital for seven months — seven months! — which leaves me speechless, not to mention downright scared.

I'm even more terrified when Peter tells me that Bed 3, on the other side of him, which is also empty at the moment, is normally occupied by Jim, *who has been in here for over a year.*

But suddenly everyone brightens as a tea trolley enters the ward pushed by a formidable lady in a grey housecoat.

"'Bout time, gal. Thought you'd forgotten us," shouts Peter cheerfully.

The tea lady is Babs, a Geordie, who obviously relishes the banter.

"Sit yourself up then, Peter. You can't have your tea lying down, you lazy devil, now can you? I've even got some biscuits for you today, though I don't know why I bother."

I make the instant and very wise decision never to get on the wrong side of Babs, though it's a close run thing when I ask for coffee instead of tea (look of disapproval) and then refuse sugar (surprise) and a biscuit (disbelief). Peter takes four sugars and two shortbread fingers and Babs beams approval. Perhaps the rule is to take what you can when it is offered as the supply of biscuits is limited and irregular, though the real scarcity turns out to be fresh fruit, which is odd for a hospital where the mantra is to encourage a more healthy diet.

I now have a table on castors which I can slide over the bed. This is quite a luxury and I might just get through the day without spilling food down my chest.

I also notice that there is a sign above my bed with my name on it and also the news that I have a "Dedicated Nurse" called Sally.

Though I never did find out what a Dedicated Nurse does, as Sally is on holiday when I arrive in Birch Ward and only returns to work on the day I am discharged.

When the family arrive late that afternoon, they all say I am looking so much better, speaking much more clearly and, above all, I'm reasonably clean.

Alyson presses me on what the doctors have said and doesn't seem to believe that I haven't seen one yet. What about the CT scan? And what came of the blood samples that were taken on my arrival in Accident and Emergency?

I have no answers for her. For God's sake, I've managed to have an assisted shower. Isn't that enough for one day?

The two empty beds are filled as "bedtime", which appears to be around 7.30p.m., approaches. On the opposite side of the Bay, between the dapper Brian and the comatose John, is Ged, who looks to be the youngest of us. He cannot speak or walk, but can manoeuvre his wheelchair with staggering speed and seems able to get in and out of bed using his arms and upper body strength, without help from the nurses.

The other inmate who has finally appeared is another matter.

This is Jim, who occupies the bed next to Peter's and he too moves around in a wheelchair. (As does Peter when he leaves his bed.) But unlike Ged, Jim has to be helped with everything. In fact, for several days I am convinced he too has lost the power of speech, but in fact he has simply chosen not to talk. Each morning he is woken by nurses who wash, shave and dress him and get him into his wheelchair. He then disappears for the entire day, returning only after dinner when he is "rounded up" before bedtime. I am to discover that he spends his day sitting about a foot away from a television in the dining room, clutching the remote control, although never changing channels. He watches whatever BBC 1 has to offer, from about 7.45a.m. until 7.30p.m. every day, without saying a word to anyone. He appears to have no visitors and does not seem to be undergoing any sort of therapy, and Peter has told me he's been there for over a year.

As the lights start going out and the ward quietens down for the night, Peter lays out a formidable array of tablets on his table and begins to "self-medicate".

I have drawn the screens around my bed so that my reading light does not annoy anyone. I am determined to get past page 17 in the Gore Vidal and, anyway, there's no way I'm going to sleep this early.

Peter asks me to pull back one side of the screen curtains. He says he doesn't mind the light, but he needs a clear view of the D Bay clock on the wall opposite as he has to take one of his many pills at exactly 8p.m. because he's been told to. He is to tell me this every night, and every night he falls asleep and is snoring away by 7.50p.m. Every morning as soon as he wakes up, Peter has to take the forgotten pill, amidst much muttering and swearing, some 11 hours late. Why he doesn't take it with the six or seven others he seems to take after dinner I just do not know, but I don't think it is appropriate for me, the new boy, to suggest that.

A nurse I haven't seen before arrives to take my blood pressure again. This is now a twice daily ritual and I'm getting used to it, although I still don't have the sense to ask what it all means or why it needs to be taken. I assume that the nurses know what they are doing and that it is all for my benefit in the long run. I am still, five days after the stroke, in a state of shock about it all.

Interpreting blood pressure readings

Blood pressure (**Bp**) readings are expressed as two figures measured in millimetres of mercury, written as **mmHg**. (Hg is the chemical symbol for mercury).

The two figures are said as one **over** the other. The first figure (the highest) is the **systolic** reading, which measures the pressure when the heart beats to pump the blood. The second figure (the lower one) is the **diastolic** reading, which is a measurement of the pressure when the heart relaxes.

A Bp reading is thus a systolic measurement over a diastolic one.

A "normal", healthy blood pressure reading would regularly be **below 140mmHg over 90mmHG** or 140/90. If your readings are regularly between 140/90 and 160/95, then you could be borderline **hypertensive** and if above 160/95, you definitely have high blood pressure which needs treating.

Some doctors regard the **systolic** figure as the more important warning indicator when it comes to stroke, but usually both **systolic** and **diastolic** measurements are considered together in a diagnosis.

In the 1998 Health Survey in England, it was found that 42% of men and 33% of women had high blood pressure; i.e. higher than 140/90.

Better control of blood pressure could prevent thousands of medical emergencies — one estimate is the prevention of 40,000 strokes alone — as well as disabilities, and produce immense savings for the Health Service.

Then another nurse does the rounds asking each inmate how many "bottles" they require for the night. I am totally perplexed and have no idea what she's talking about until she shows me one of the banana shaped bottles made out of compressed cardboard, which look big enough to hold a couple of pints of liquid.

These bottles fit in the metal hoops attached to the side of the bed frame so they are within easy reach of the patient.

"I thought they were for the wine coolers," I say, which I think is pretty funny but which produces a totally blank stare from the nurse, who stands there waiting for an answer, so I tell her none, thank you.

Peter takes three. It turns out to be not enough.

CHAPTER
FOUR

People in the Tottenham Court Road would pay good money for this

It is not a peaceful night and sleep eludes me.

I struggle with *The Golden Age*, which seems to be getting heavier every time I open it, but I still can't concentrate enough to decode the words. And then the snoring starts, rising from each bed in turn as if the occupant is part of an orchestra tuning up before a performance.

At first it's quite amusing in a surreal way and gives me the giggles — guilty giggles as I know I would probably be joining in if I could get to sleep. But after two hours, the joke has worn thin. The noise level has reached that of a rolling artillery barrage and nobody seems to be running low on ammunition. I've never heard anything quite like it, but then I've never shared a bedroom with five other men before.

But worse is to come. As if on cue, the snoring level drops almost to a whisper so that the noise of someone (I can't tell who) using his night time bottle can clearly be heard by all. And where one goes in that area, others are sure to follow so that within minutes everyone is reaching for a bottle (even though they seem to be asleep) and the sound of rushing streams is so loud I feel I am camping next to a waterfall.

I try to hold a pillow over my ears, but this is hardly practical with only one arm working. I even think of the headphones above my bed, which I've already discovered don't work as far as receiving radio stations goes. Perhaps they will work as earplugs. They don't and I am convinced I will never ever get to sleep again, and at precisely that point, I do.

Mornings in Birch Ward begin around 7 a.m. with the pre-breakfast (thank goodness) ritual collection of "bottles". Peter has indeed filled three and so too has old John in the corner but he still asks the nurse attending if he can go to the toilet. It is the first time I have heard him speak but the nurse gives a resigned shrug and sighs heavily as if she'd gone through this many times before.

"Come on then," she tells him encouragingly. "Do you need a chair or are you going to try under your own steam?"

John indicates that he wants to walk and the nurse helps him sit up and swing his legs over the edge of the bed. Once in that position, she tells him not to move while she gets his dressing gown and slippers from his locker on the other side of his bed.

But John doesn't listen, or wait. He staggers unsteadily to his feet and I think at first that he's off balance and about to fall flat on his face, but he is only getting himself into position. Once his feet are planted firmly apart, he closes his eyes, allows himself a big smile, and empties his bladder there and then, the stain spreading over his pyjama trousers. After seeing all the full bottles he has produced in the night, I am just staggered he has any fluid left in him. The nurse says something under her breath and, shaking her head, starts to draw the screens. Nobody says anything, though we are all awake now, and I suspect that this is John's standard early morning ritual. (It is.)

Breakfast comes round on a trolley pushed by the formidable Babs, who can offer us a choice of Corn Flakes or sliced white bread and jam. She apologises for the fact that she cannot provide toast, but says there may be porridge tomorrow.

I have already realised that a patient's reaction to hospital food, rightly the butt of so many jokes, is an indicator of how long you have "been in". The longer you are an in-patient, the more institutionalised you become and the food becomes something you accept. In my time in hospital, I heard far more complaints from long term patients about meals being two or three minutes *late* than about the quality of the food.

I am sure my mother would have said that if you were well enough to complain about the food, you were probably well enough not to be in hospital, and I take this as a sign that I must be improving as long as I keep complaining.

One morning, Babs has a bunch of bananas on her trolley, which I discover is a one-a-week treat. I cause quite a stir by asking for one to chop into a bowl of Corn Flakes. Babs agrees to this with deep suspicion and only on condition that she uses the knife. There is a genuine puzzlement all round at my constant refusal to take sugar with anything as the average seems to be around four spoonfuls per cup of whatever hot drink is going. This isn't a health thing, although I am overweight, it's just that I haven't taken sugar in tea or coffee for 30 years. When we do get porridge for breakfast, I ask if there is any honey and a frantic but futile search ensues through a box of individual portion pots of jam and marmalade. My neighbour Peter comes to my rescue. He has about half a dozen small pots of honey stashed in his locker from the days when there must have been a honey glut.

Hypertension

Because of its name, hypertension is often thought to be caused by tension or stress and telling somebody to "watch your blood pressure" when they are getting angry goes back to days of the Music Hall.

Stress *can* raise your **Bp**, but only temporarily. It soon drops back to its usual level. The problem for 16 million adults in the UK is that their "usual" level is too high to begin with.

Hypertension has been called "the silent killer" which strikes without warning, as there are no obvious symptoms before something drastic happens. It is sometimes referred to as an **asymptomatic** condition.

Just to confuse things, there are two categories of hypertension.

Essential or **Primary** hypertension is the most common, accounting for almost 90% of all cases of high blood pressure. Doctors are unable to identify a single cause, though the usual suspects are likely to be smoking, obesity, bad diet and hereditary factors.

Secondary hypertension is when high blood pressure is caused by an underlying condition such as kidney disease, a thyroid condition or drug or alcohol misuse, which themselves exhibit medical symptoms.

Only in very severe cases of Primary Hypertension could there be symptoms such as dizziness, flushed face, nervousness, fatigue, nose bleeds and headaches, but in the majority of cases, the consequences of high blood pressure arrive without warning.

The only defence is to be aware of your Bp — *get to know your Bp numbers and try and control them.*

Ignorance, they say, is no defence in law and it certainly isn't when it comes to hypertension.

That morning, I get my first taste of physiotherapy, although it takes a long time for it to sink in that I have passed from "acute" to "rehabilitation".

A young, muscular blonde in her early twenties, wearing a green t-shirt and tracksuit bottoms, appears at my bedside just as the smiling nurse Sarah finishes taking my blood pressure. Her name badge says "Eloise" and she asks if I would like to start physiotherapy as soon as her colleague gets here.

I say sure, as I have nothing else planned, and her colleague turns out to be a pretty, slim brunette called Roxanne, who looks about 19 and speaks with a languid Australian drawl. I immediately christen them Bambi and Thumper and physiotherapy turns out to be quite fun as the pair of them, with their arms round my waist, walk me up and down the corridor to see how much power I have in my left leg.

They seem quite pleased with that and we then move into a small gymnasium at the end of the ward I haven't explored yet, for some bending, stretching and straining. Bambi is confident that my leg will have full power back fairly soon, though I have to concentrate on consciously lifting my left foot to avoid tripping and scuffing.

I tell her that my main problem is my limp left arm and the fact that I keep bumping in to door frames. She says we'll work on that tomorrow and she'll give me some exercises to do. Then Bambi and Thumper put an arm each around me and as we go back down the corridor I suggest we do *Putting On The Ritz*, but they are both too young to know what I mean. So young, they probably haven't even seen the *Young Frankenstein* version, which in my state would be just about all I could manage.

No sooner do the girls leave me at my bed side than someone else comes a-calling. I am in demand today. This is the Occupational Therapist, who pencils me in for a session tomorrow, though I have no idea what an Occupational Therapist does, or how she can help me, though as she leaves she says that my speech seems fine, so I won't be needing a Speech Therapist. I suppose that too means progress of some sort.

The clock ticks round to lunchtime and Babs, a woman you wouldn't want to argue with, suggests that I have it in the dining room. So I do, although with some trepidation as not only do I have to *find* the dining room, I will have to do something in public for the first time and not just in front of nurses, who have seen every type of weird behaviour possible.

The dining room is about 20 feet down the corridor, beyond another small ward called C Bay, which I discover to my surprise contains female patients I had no idea were there.

I pick an empty table, but am quickly joined by Peter, who pulls up in his wheelchair and attacks his lunch with a will. He has developed a technique of using his knife and fork together, almost as chopsticks, and it is incredibly efficient. He clears his plate before I have worked out that I can't grip with my left hand and switch to right hand eating, using the fork only. And then he's finished his dessert and is wheeling himself away, his lunch having taken all of about three minutes, and I am left alone again, though not for long.

I am joined by three ladies from C Bay. One is in her eighties, in a wheelchair and doesn't speak at all. One is younger than me, also in a wheelchair, and has obviously had a really bad stroke: she cannot speak and it clearly drives her mad trying, nor can she control her right arm which jerks and shakes with a life of its own. The third woman introduces herself as Diane, a retired teacher — possibly a headmistress.

She tells me she has had special dispensation to make fairy cakes in the Birch Ward kitchen and they will be served with tea that afternoon. She scoffs at the fact that she has to have nurses watching her in case she burns herself. Then she lowers her voice and says "They're really worried about me messing up their pristine kitchen."

I whisper that I didn't know they had a working kitchen, judging by the food, and she says "Quite."

Over the next week or so, I get on very well with Diane, cooperating with her on the Daily Telegraph crossword, praising her fairy cakes, discussing books, meeting her visitors (all former pupils) nearly all of whom had trekked over two hundred miles to see her. And then I don't see her for a few days. I don't know why, but she's just not around in the usual places and at the time I don't think about it too much. But a week after I am discharged, I pay a flying visit to Birch Ward with chocolates for the nurses, and there is Diane in a wheelchair. She looks 20 years older and totally lost. I make a point of going up to her and asking how she is, but it's clear she has no idea who I am or why I'm speaking to her. The nurse pushing her chair just shakes her head sadly.

That night, Alyson brings me a bag of apples, clean clothes and more get well messages, including one from the Irish thriller writer John Connolly who claims I am

"Proof that only the good die young". Guy brings me a jam jar full of his patented balsamic vinegar salad dressing, which does indeed do wonders for the limp lettuce and grated carrots that is my salad for dinner. The genial Babs offers to keep it in the kitchen fridge, although she looks at the black, oily liquid with shards of garlic floating in it, with deep suspicion.

Guy's Salad Dressing
Crush then finely chop a clove of garlic and mix to a paste with salt, black pepper and just a pinch of sugar. Add to apple balsamic vinegar and good olive oil.

The weather forecast is for snow and I tell Aly not to bother coming if the roads are too bad, but she scoffs at the idea and says I'm much better off in Birch Ward than I would be working out on a frozen archaeological site.

It begins to sink in slowly that the excavation I was working on will be finished in about two weeks, and I will be unemployed for the first time in my life.

To distract me, Aly says that a load of books have arrived at home — books for me to review for my monthly column in the *Birmingham Post* — but I tell her to hang on to them as I've still got some way to go with the Gore Vidal.

Amazingly, I do get beyond page 17 that night (if only to the bottom of page 18), with a supreme effort of concentration, considering the background distractions. Everyone is in bed and, except for me, asleep by

8p.m. Jim has been forcibly removed from in front of the television and wheeled back to his bed. Only as she is getting him into bed does the nurse notice that he is still holding the remote control.

With D Bay in darkness except for my reading light, the snoring orchestra tunes up and builds to a window rattling level. Then there is another noise, which only I seem to notice: music. Jim has fallen asleep whilst listening to the radio and his headphones have dislodged themselves. If I can hear it at the other end of the ward, he must have the volume up to 11. It may be this which wakes old John opposite for he starts calling plaintively for a nurse.

Nobody else stirs, despite the snoring, the radio and the increasingly loud cries of "Nurse, nurse!" and so I press my panic button as John by now sounds genuinely in distress.

An agency nurse is on Twilight Shift duty. She is tall, thin, blonde and very severe and appears suddenly at my bedside snapping "What is it?" at me, despite John's quite audible cries for help. I tell her I am fine, but worried about old John. She gives me a look of utter disdain and goes over to John's bed to discover he has decided not to use the cardboard bottles tonight and so his bed has to be stripped and he has to be washed while sitting in a chair.

When finally she pulls back the screens and leaves she shoots me the filthiest possible look as if it was all my fault, so, with nothing to lose, I ask her if she can turn off Jim's radio, which I can still hear.

"I can't hear a radio," she says.

Needless to say, this humourless agency nurse, who only worked evening and night shifts, rapidly became known as "Nurse Ratchett". Not once did I see her smile or hear her say a sociable word to a patient or any of the other nurses. Come to think of it, I never actually saw her in daylight . . . She reminded me of a faded British film starlet from the 1960s who was still waiting for a decent role. She has stuck in my mind for the simple reason that she was the ONLY nurse, male or female, I came across who did not go out of their way to make sure their patients were both comfortable and comforted.

The next morning brings more strength and flexing exercises with Bambi and Thumper, both of whom are happy with the return of feeling and function in my left leg, though they tell me (again) to lift my foot when I walk to avoid scuffing. I am not aware that I am scuffing.

I am more worried about my left arm, as I have realised that while archaeology may be out of the question for the immediate future, unless I can get my arm working, writing will be too, not to mention everyday skills like tying shoelaces, opening bottles of wine and driving. (Three things which just happened to spring to mind, though I have not tried to do any of them since being in hospital.)

Bambi gives me two new exercises for the arm. The first is simply to raise the arm with the palm held flat, almost like a street beggar asking for your small change.

I call this one the "Big Issue" exercise. The second involves placing the left hand on the left hip and then turning the forearm out at 90 degrees and then bringing the palm back in a slow arc. This becomes known as the "Gay Air Hostess" exercise.

They are meant to be delicate movement control exercises and at first they seem silly and ineffective. Then I see other patients, including Brian in D Bay, practising them when they think no one is looking, but they do seem to work and I take great glee in managing, the next day, to tie a shoelace — even if I do fall over and crash into my locker whilst bending down to do it. After 48 hours, I can actually hold a fork at the dinner table. I cannot use it very well, but I can hold it. Another milestone.

About an hour after my physio session, Bambi and Thumper come into D Bay looking for Ged, but he has disappeared again. He hates physiotherapy so much he has become a regular Scarlet Pimpernel and is by now an expert at evading Bambi and Thumper.

Deprived of one victim, they ask me if they can try out an experiment which might just help my arm. I have to try and flex my shoulders so that my shoulder blades stick out of my back. There is no problem with the right one, but the left just doesn't respond, so Bambi and Thumper manipulate it until it does and then quickly bind my arm to my side with yards of surgical tape. Thus bound, but not gagged, they gently lay me face down on the bed and begin to knead the muscles in my neck and spine.

It is remarkably pleasant, though I'm not sure if it is doing any good, and there is a surreal look to it all; me tied up with tape and two attractive young girls knocking seven bells out of me.

Between gasps for air, I manage to say: "There are people down the Tottenham Court Road would pay good money for this."

Now given the circumstances, I thought that was one of my better efforts, but neither Bambi nor Thumper seemed amused. And, as it turns out, that was the last session of physiotherapy I received.

Physiotherapy

Not that I'm complaining about this. I think I had showed all the signs of recovering most of the use of my left leg and arm and the physiotherapists had other, more seriously disabled patients to tend to. Some stroke survivors go on having extensive physio for many months, if not years, after their strokes, but much depends on the provision of physiotherapists locally. It is generally accepted that even small amounts of physiotherapy earlier on can have hugely beneficial effects. It is also generally accepted that there are not enough physiotherapists employed by the NHS.

Occupational Therapy, the next day, turns out to be depressingly unchallenging, I am delighted to say.

There is a very nice lady and a student observer in a room stuffed with toys. I have to prove I can put square things in square holes, pick up ridiculously small beads and do a written test. All this — the three of us agree — I do superbly well; but that's because I'm naturally right handed. I point out that it is my limp and lifeless *left* hand which isn't working.

But we press on with the tests. I have to draw a clock face (a quite important test of spatial awareness, though I didn't know that), so I do a digital one: 14:10 which makes the Therapist laugh. Then she asks me to write a list of 12 colours, so I do: red, yellow, crimson, amber, orange, silver, grey, scarlet, blue, gold, purple and pink and then I explain that these are all colours mentioned in the titles of novels starring Travis McGee by one of my heroes, the writer John D. MacDonald. Somehow, she is not as impressed by this as I am.

The Therapist tries to encourage me by saying I should be pleased at my recovery so far, after just a week. When I think about some of the people I have met here in Birch Ward who have suffered much more than I have and in some cases for over a year, I realise how lucky I have been. But when she says I should be patient and let things take their course, I snap at her, saying I have to get my left hand working again so at least I can write again.

In truth, my anger is generated by fear more then anything and I realise it is unfair to take it out on anyone else. But the Therapist does say she will find a computer keyboard to practise on and she's as good as her word.

Each evening, after 6p.m., I am allowed to use the computer in the gymnasium. I don't have a password so I can't hack into the hospital intranet and mess up the medical records, of course, but I can write in Microsoft Word to my heart's content.

At last I am doing something constructive towards my rehabilitation, or so I think for about two minutes. Then I realise that the computer keyboard has a life of its own and is producing absolute gibberish on the screen. It doesn't stay there for long, as the computer regularly deletes everything — and then will suddenly repeat a key, \\\\\\\\\\\\\\\\\\\\\ like that, for no good reason. It is just my luck to get the only NHS computer in need of an exorcism.

But it is me who needs the exorcism — or rather my limp left hand, which is twitching like a landed fish over the keys in that crucial bottom left corner of the keyboard, the ones marked Caps Lock, Ctrl and Alt, the one with the arrow Shift symbol and the one bearing the Microsoft logo. Hit any of them with my left paw and it seems I can ruin the sentence I have laboriously pecked out with one or two fingers of my right hand; and I do hit them — every time I breathe out or so it seems.

After an hour and almost weeping with frustration, I give up.

Halfway back to D Bay, in the middle of the corridor by the Reception Desk, I suddenly start crying for real.

It is just as well that Aly and the kids have been and gone for the day as I wouldn't want to scare them by letting them see me like this. And yet that night, which marked the bottom of my despair, also saw me resolving to get better and get out of there.

It is as I scuff my way into D Bay, feeling very sorry for myself, and survey my surroundings that I decide that something must be done. My fellow inmates are all neatly tucked up in bed, though it is not yet 8p.m., and as I look around me, I divide D Bay into two teams: the hopefuls and the lost hopers.

There is not much poor Ged can do about his condition. He has had by far the most seriously disabling stroke and cannot speak. But he seems the most cheerful of all of us, refusing help wherever possible and he is certainly independent once in his wheelchair thanks to the upper body strength he has developed. I don't know what his chances are of regaining some percentage of his former life, but he certainly fits into my hopefuls team. He plays a game with the physiotherapists: if they can catch him, he'll do the exercises, though they usually have to find him first for he wanders all over the hospital. When he has visitors, he is the life and soul of the bedside party, holding forth with expansive gestures and long and involved stories and jokes, although it all comes out as "Spah-da, spah-da", yet his enthusiasm somehow makes it understandable.

One Saturday night we watch *Match of the Day* together and we both agree most forcefully that a particular referee is as spah-da-ing blind as a spah-da-ing bat.

The normally quiet and polite Brian is becoming more talkative and complains at the slightest excuse that he feels he is ready to go home, but can't do so without the consultant's consent, and nobody has seen the consultant so far this week. As time goes by and still the consultant does not appear, he grows more grumpy and more determined than ever to get away. Another hopeful, definitely.

The lost hopers have done just that — lost all hope of living an independent life and resigned themselves to institutionalised care.

Old John has, to my untrained eye, given up completely. He cries out for nurses to take him to the toilet and yet fails to get there in time on every occasion, whether he is walking or in a chair. He has also been calling out plaintively during the night for someone to "rub my feet" and cannot wash or feed himself. During the second week of my stay in Birch Ward, John is moved out — in a wheelchair with his spare clothes in a bag across his knees — "to a home". There is no one to see him off or accompany him, apart from the ambulance driver.

Jim, the anti-social television addict, becomes even more withdrawn and, when he is forced to leave the TV screen, he has his headphones on or a small transistor radio clamped to his ear to shut out the world. Neither Jim nor John have any visitors while I am there, but one day he is collected by a nurse and taken out for the day. This turns out to be an advance visit to a long term care home, or so the ward nurses tell us, to which he will be moving shortly. On his return, he says not a word but wheels himself into the dining room and parks his chair in front of the television.

Peter is the one I feel most sorry for. He looks the worst of us. His skin is blotched and flaking, he is prone to bouts of violent vomiting (to which one of the young student nurses, Louisa, says: "Now, Peter, you know I don't do sick"), unsteady at best on his feet and subject to bouts of violent depression. And yet he tries to do things for himself, even if, as I suspect, he has convinced himself he will never get better. His lack of hope is sad, but what is truly frightening is the way in which he has institutionalised himself. He has his own wheelchair — it even has his name written on it in felt-tip pen — and he throws a tantrum if it is not available because someone else has used it. He sits up in bed when his internal radar tells him the tea trolley is coming round, always has four sugars in his tea and any biscuits on offer, which he stores in his locker rather than eats. It is a grab-it-if-it's-offered attitude, which is understandable, but when the tea trolley is five minutes late it is as if his human rights have been infringed.

On one occasion I do genuinely shock him by going to the nurses' lounge and making myself a cup of instant coffee, which I bring back to D Bay.

"I don't think they like you doing that," Peter warns me.

"They can bill me," I say, and Peter looks appalled.

Shortly after this, I am caught in the lounge at 5.30 a.m. with another coffee, by now sailing past page 117 of *The Golden Age*, by the duty Sister, who begins to berate me. I point out that I still cannot sleep through the night amid the D Bay snoring chorus and so I've come in here to read. Then I realise she's yelling about the coffee and I don't endear myself by saying stupidly "But it's only instant, it's not like *real* coffee".

But in fact she's having a go at me for ignoring the sign which says that (stroke) patients should not attempt to use the kettle unsupervised.

In all his time there, I don't think Peter ever made it as far as that lounge, but if he had, he would have obeyed that notice as if his life depended upon it.

It was seeing the lost hope in Peter more than anything else which persuaded me that I was going to get better, no matter what it took. The prospect of being like him in seven months' time — it was seven months since his stroke — was simply too frightening to contemplate.

CHAPTER
FIVE

The Great Escape

The first part of my escape plan is to reclaim as much normalcy as possible; to do things I would normally do and not just sit around waiting for something to happen or a bolt out of the blue to make me fit again. I must not lie there and accept it. I must not play by the rules the stroke wants to impose on me.

In my first days in The Twilight Zone, Alyson had smuggled in my mobile phone, but as there are signs everywhere in the hospital warning that phone signals could interfere with medical equipment, I have not even switched it on. But from D Bay's window I can see people in the snow covered car park below using them, so I decide to join them.

Hiding the phone in the pocket of my dressing gown, I walk through Birch Ward and out on to the stairwell without being stopped, searched or questioned by anyone (though there is no reason why anyone should — patients are free to move about and visitors come and go all day).

I experience a great feeling of accomplishment, having got out of D Bay and then out of Birch Ward entirely, but as I am on the top floor, there is nowhere else to go but down and so I do, confidently taking the stairs rather than the lift. Holding tightly on to the hand rail fixed in the wall, I lower myself like a mountaineer down two short flights until I find I am on the first floor where the stairwell has one of the biggest vending machines I have ever seen, fully stocked with crisps and chocolate bars of all known flavours and brands. I immediately kick myself for not bringing any cash with me, as Alyson has left me a pile of change for newspapers and the phone box on the ward (which still isn't working, as it is full and won't take any more coins).

It never occurs to me, at least not then, that everything in that machine is loaded either with salt or sugar (probably both) — the very things we overweight hypertensives will be warned against.

Down two more flights and I'm on the ground floor and there are automatic doors leading to the outside world and I've made it. I am standing in the hospital car park. I'm in pyjamas, dressing gown and slippers and it is snowing. I suddenly realise I feel very cold, very foolish and I have my mobile phone clutched in my right hand but I cannot remember for the life of me who it was I wanted to call.

There is no one else in sight. In fact, the snow is coming down so thickly I can't see the main hospital about 50 yards away. Then a car looking for a parking slot goes into a skid and slides sideways, narrowly avoiding hitting one already parked. I realise it would be a terrible irony to survive a stroke and then get run over in the hospital car park, and so I head back inside, grateful for once that the temperature in the Gainsborough Wing is close to that of a greenhouse at Kew Gardens.

The ascent of the stairwell takes about four times longer than the descent, but I finally make it, bathed in sweat and incredibly pleased with myself. Going up and down those stairs at least once a day, sometimes twice, becomes my personal exercise regime. On the ground floor there is a little shop run by volunteer "Friends of the Hospital" which sells sweets, snacks, fruit, flowers and newspapers to both patients and visitors. It gives me the perfect excuse to use those stairs: in the mornings to get a newspaper and then in the afternoon to buy some sweets for the kids when they visit (though I try and drop the hint that they are supposed to bring me gifts).

I don't tell anyone I'm doing this, and certainly no other Birch Ward patient is, but as I am no longer being offered physiotherapy, it is the only exercise I get.

Some days I get dressed for these excursions and even venture over into the main hospital where there is a bigger shop which also sells second hand books and I even find an ex-library edition of a William McIlvanney novel I had not heard of, which cheers me up no end. Returning to Birch Ward after one of these jaunts, I am mistaken for a visitor to the ward by a family of real visitors looking for a patient in a private room. I hadn't known there were private rooms, so I take them to the nurses' station where Bill, one of the senior male nurses, says they've been looking for me to take my blood pressure and would I mind getting back in my bed.

One morning the cheeky young nurse — Louisa (a short brunette with bags of attitude) — announces loudly:

"Come on, Mike. Let's do some drugs!"

Then, under her breath: "It's only aspirin, I'm afraid."

Nurse Bill explains that I will probably be taking a small daily dose of aspirin (75mg, sometimes known as "half-aspirin" or, in America, "baby aspirin") as well as other drugs for the rest of my life and they need to see if I can cope with "self-medication". This is nothing more than opening the bottle and taking a small tablet once a day, but I am watched like a hawk for the first few days to make sure I can manage, or, more likely, to make sure I don't forget.

Reducing high blood pressure

If your blood pressure is not too high, **non-pharmacological treatments** can be effective — which is a very fancy way of saying you don't always need to take drugs. These treatments revolve around diet and what is nowadays known as "lifestyle".

Family doctors are often criticised for failing to explain to patients how to change their lifestyle, but then very few patients want "boring" advice about losing weight and stopping smoking as it involves giving up things they like. A far easier prescription would be a magic pill which does it all for you even though one does not, as yet, exist.

Reducing the body's sodium intake and increasing the potassium intake is important for blood pressure. This is a very fancy way of saying take less **salt** and eat more **fruit**.

Victims with high cholesterol levels have to be more careful and take advice on reducing their fat intake. **Statins**, the drugs given to lower cholesterol, have been proved to work better in conjunction with a diet.

Exercise is always mentioned as being good for hypertension, with even as little as a 30 minute brisk walk every day making a difference.

Relaxing — simply taking it easy — has no real effect, though some practitioners maintain that, whilst **Yoga** won't actually lower high blood pressure, it is good for maintaining a steady level once it has come down.

Neither alcohol nor smoking have long term effects on blood pressure directly, but smoking can clog up the arteries (which does have an effect) and of course can be linked to lung and heart disease. Alcohol actually gives some protection against heart disease, but doesn't help if you are trying to lose weight.

I begin to press the nurses for more information on what the future might hold for me, though it still doesn't occur to me to ask about my blood pressure, which is ritually being measured twice a day.

I'm told that the results of my CT or CAT scan are now known, though of course the consultant hasn't seen them because he's off sick.

The Computerised Tomography (or Computed Axial Tomography) scan, has confirmed that I suffered a blood clot on the right side of the brain, which had affected the left side of my body. In technical terms, I learn that this was "a right internal capsule infarct".

No one is saying what might have caused it, but Nurse Bill says the smoking "can't have helped" and asks if anyone has said anything about giving up? I tell him not officially, though I haven't had a cigarette for 11 days, eight hours and 43 minutes — not that I was counting, of course. He suggests nicotine patches and later that day he brings me a supply, but I don't actually start to use them until after I am discharged.

Although I had smoked about 20 cigarettes a day for over 25 years, I had always associated smoking with concentration on a piece of work, not relaxation. I could quite happily watch a film or a play without a cigarette and often go an entire weekend without one, but back at work in the office, or sitting at home in from of a computer screen or the blank sheet of paper in a typewriter, I would automatically reach for my cigarettes and lighter. I always grabbed a cigarette when the phone rang, something which used to drive Alyson crazy. It is her threat to break my fingers if she finds me with a cigarette which will be far more effective than nicotine patches in the long run.

During the family's evening visit, I tell Aly about the CT scan and she agrees to email one of our American friends, Ray Daniloff. Ray is a professor of Audiology at the University of Texas, and teaches people to be speech therapists. Both personally and professionally he has experience of heart problems and strokes and has been emailing for a diagnosis since it happened.

I tell Aly to reply with the words "right side — clot, not bleed" only, which she does and he responds with: "You have, my friend, avoided a very bad bullet".

I approach all the senior nurses in turn and ask what I should expect in terms of recovery. The general pattern seems to be that if I am going to recover, I will reacquire the "big moves" fairly quickly, within two weeks, which I already have. I can walk, talk and go to the toilet unaided. Compared to the majority of D Bay, I'm there under false pretences.

Then I am to expect the finer movements to come back or be relearned in the next three months or so. After that recovery will slow to an almost undetectable pace for anything up to two years. One Sister, Annie, warns me that stroke victims never really "recover" in that damaged brain cells remain damaged, but the brain learns to do things a different way and there may be things I did before which I will have to learn to do again from scratch.

How long does recovery take?

There is an understandable sensitivity about how long it takes to recover from a stroke, where recovery is possible.

I have read and been told that "survivors make all the recovery they are going to make in the first six months".

I have also read that "most recovery takes place during the first year to 18 months, but many people continue to improve over a much longer period".

I myself continue to improve both physically and certainly mentally, almost three years post-stroke. It is impossible to lay down hard and fast rules. Just as no two strokes are exactly the same, no two recoveries are.

I am told by Moira, the ward administrator, that I will have to give up driving for at least a month — something I had not thought about at all — and watch my diet. I am given a pamphlet produced by the Stroke Association entitled "Eat A Rainbow" which urges me to eat more fruit and vegetables by colour coding them. Some 24 examples are given of healthy fruit and vegetables to "fill your plate with colour". Only two — tomatoes and peas — have featured on the Birch Ward menus during my stay there.

All the staff seek reassurance that I will be able to cope at home, or rather, that I have someone to look after me. I assure them I can and I have, and the house does not need any major alterations or equipment such as stair lifts or ramps for wheelchairs (which I haven't used since the day I arrived in Birch) or grab rails or safety devices in the kitchen.

The impact on relationships

In all these exchanges, I am asked if I have a wife or partner who can care for me, yet not once does anyone ask my wife Alyson if she can cope with me.

Two years on, as I start to meet and work with stroke survivors, I notice that one of the questions most frequently asked is "Are you and your wife still together?"

Stroke cuts a terrible swathe through peoples' lives in many ways.

Brian, back in D Bay, is getting more and more angry because he thinks the staff are dragging their heels about his discharge. He is in fact in better shape than I am, but because he's a retired bachelor, the nurses are worried he will return home to a cold house (it is still snowing out in the real world) with no food and no one to watch out for him.

I try and calm Brian by saying that there is nothing the staff can do without the say-so of the consultant, from whom a visit is promised any day now. Whilst there is an on call junior doctor for the Ward, there seems to be only one consultant covering stroke patients — and he's been ill, probably from mixing with all those sick people, I quip to cheer Brian up, but it doesn't work.

One day there is a rumour on the Ward that the consultant will do his rounds that afternoon and poor Brian gets dressed and packs his bags, ready to leave at the first mention of the word "outpatient". As dinner time approaches, he moves his bags off the foot of his bed and gets his pyjamas out, resigning himself to another day of confinement.

Every evening I retreat to the small gymnasium where the staff have left the computer on for me. After several days of pure frustration I am now managing to pick out whole sentences with something close to punctuation. I am writing anything which comes into my head, trying to remember famous opening lines from books, or passages from my own novels. I was working on a new novel when I was so rudely interrupted by the stroke, but I don't even attempt to do anything on that for the simple, and rather worrying, reason that I cannot for the life of me remember where I was in the story.

Something does emerge, though, almost subconsciously. I begin to write a series of notes, as if they were transcripts of messages, detailing the plans for a mass escape from "Stalag Luft Birch". These include bribing Babs (the tea lady) to keep watch for "the Goons" while work continues on Tom, Dick and Harry — three tunnels going out from the Sluice Room, D Bay and the patients' lounge. I sign them all "Big X" and each night leave them, saved, on the screen in the hope that whoever comes round turning off the computers at night will read them. They may not have been hysterically funny, but they cheered me up — especially the one where Big X reported his shock at finding that Birch Ward was on the second floor and so ordered the abandonment of the tunnels and revived an earlier plan to build a glider in the loft out of those pressed cardboard urinary bottles.

One even had a complete, detailed timetable of the guards' duty rota as they "patrolled the perimeter" and called for suggestions on how to distract the guard dogs while we made a dash across the car park in wheelchairs, and, using the slope for momentum, got up enough speed to "jump the wire", as Steve McQueen did on a motorbike in the film.

My escape plans were never mentioned by the staff so I suppose nobody ever looked at the screen before switching off for the night. It was probably just as well or they might have called in the psychiatrist.

Eventually, the Great Escape happens for real. The consultant makes his rounds early one afternoon. And where am I? I've gone walkabout in the main hospital where the League of Friends Shop is having a book sale and I have acquired a "Flashman" novel by the great George Macdonald Fraser for 10p.

So I'm looking pretty pleased with myself as I climb the stairs back to Birch Ward, though nowhere near as pleased as Brian who is standing by his bed packing his bags again. He can hardly wait to tell me that the consultant has been, has discharged him and he's off — out of here — offski — just as soon as he has organised a lift home. (He had obviously not thought of *how* he was going to leave when he made his break for freedom.)

Several of the nurses stop by to tell me I missed the consultant and my excuse — that there was a second hand book sale on — does not impress anyone.

But the consultant, after his initial blitzkrieg through the ward, sweeps back for mopping up operations and we meet at last.

Checking things off a clipboard, he tells me I had a right sided blood clot, but obviously I'm well on the way to recovery (obviously). The trick will be to prevent another one. He asks who my local doctor is and I tell him Dr David Milne, of the surgery in West Bergholt (the next village to where we live), and the consultant nods approvingly and says he'll write to him and I should go and see him as soon as I can. I ask what caused the stroke. He says, automatically, that "the smoking didn't help", but won't commit himself further than that.

While smoking wasn't the direct cause — hypertension or high blood pressure was — years of smoking had gummed up my arteries and blood vessels rather like water pipes acquire limescale, thus putting my blood circulation under extreme pressure.

The other "usual suspect" in these things is your cholesterol level, but mine, he says, checked out fine, so the problem is getting my blood pressure down to a respectable level and keeping it there. "You do not," he says with absolute gravitas, "want to have another one."

He does not have to tell me that twice, but he does tell me at least twice of the need for a good diet with no salt, lots of exercise, no smoking and a regime of drugs — almost certainly one or two different ones in combination plus aspirin.

Reducing salt consumption

Cutting down on my salt intake was the first piece of advice I received. It was also the most repeated advice, yet no one seemed to question the fact that hospital food was automatically supplied with extra salt to give it some taste. Despite an intense publicity campaign, salt cellars are to be found as a matter of course in most hospital dining rooms.

Once home from hospital, I began to check all the food in the house for its nutritional information labels, looking for foods with a sodium content (salt is sodium chloride) of less than 0.2 grams per 100 grams.

It is useful to bear in mind that some processed foods contain 1 gram of **sodium** per 100 grams, which is the equivalent concentration of the saltiness of the Atlantic Ocean.

Some things are obviously heavy on the salt, things like stock cubes, processed meats, soya sauce, take-aways and most fast foods. I worked out that a medium sized tin of a supermarket's own brand chicken soup had my recommended daily salt intake in one go.

Other foodstuffs are not so obvious (breakfast cereals for example) and you really need to check the labels.

Table salt can be easily replaced by Lo Salt which contains only about a third of the sodium and after a couple of days I doubt anyone could tell the difference.

And that appears to be that.

The consultant writes me a prescription for the hospital pharmacy and my box is ticked and I'm history as far as Birch Ward is concerned.

Or so I hope.

As soon as the consultant leaves I am sure there are a million questions I should have asked, but I cannot think of any. He's told me about the need to control my blood pressure and contact my GP, get some exercise, stop smoking and cut down on the salt. He hasn't said anything about alcohol, which is good, and neither has he said anything about *losing* weight, which is amazing. He has also made no mention of the appalling side effects which some of the drugs for hypertension have, all of which (and some new to medical science) I am going to discover in the coming year.

But enough carping; I'm outta there and I persuade the duty Sister to let me use the Reception Desk phone to call Alyson to tell her to come and get me, as the ward payphone still hasn't been emptied.

It is mid-afternoon and I get our answerphone as Aly will be on her way from work, picking the kids up from school en route. I leave a message which starts "Home run" — a reference to all those stiff-upper-lip British POW films where a successful escape is marked by sending a post card of Piccadilly Circus back to the camp saying just that.

A nurse sitting behind the desk looks up from her paperwork and asks sweetly if I'm Mike Ripley the writer. I'm delighted to be recognised though God knows I've dropped enough hints and left enough of my books lying about over the last few days. Then I read her name badge.

"And you're Sally Spencer, my dedicated nurse. I'm leaving now, goodbye."

We chat for a while and she tells me she's been on holiday "back home" in Dorset and do I by any chance know a crime writer called Minette Walters who lives there now? I said the name sounded familiar. But she writes such good books, Sally enthused. Well, yes she does, I admit, but I have to go and pack my things.

Back in D Bay, Brian gives me a thumbs up sign. He has had his coat on and his bags packed for about two hours by now and is still trying to arrange a lift home.

I (jokingly) say that I still intend to beat him with my escape, and although I had no idea that it would take two hours to get my prescription drugs from the hospital pharmacy, I actually do. It turns out Brian is relying on an elderly friend to come and get him, but she's been more or less snowed in and does not fancy getting the car out as it is already dark and the roads are treacherous. Seeing what it is like outside, I can't say I blame her but it means I leave Brian sitting hunched on the bed he will have to spend another night in.

About two months after our great escape, I run into Brian at the checkout of the local Sainsbury's supermarket and we ask each other how we are getting on. He is ahead of me in the queue and is attempting to put his eight-items-or-less into one of the store's carrier bags but obviously having difficulty getting one open. I take one to try and help him and find I have exactly the same problem. Our fingers will not grip the slippery plastic enough to prise the things open. The very respectable and normally mild mannered Brian begins to let rip a stream of curses and obscenities so colourful that the young cashier is obviously horrified and glances around wondering where the Security Officer is. As Brian pounds the still hermetically sealed carrier bag into the checkout, shouting obscenities, I grab his wrist and make him look at me. "Brian," I say slowly, "could you open one of these before the stroke, because I bloody well couldn't." He relaxes instantly and sees the funny side of things, thank goodness.

Peter is the only other patient in situ. Old John has been transferred to a care home and his bed taken by an emphysema patient who had a stroke *whilst* in hospital for treatment, and is on a bewildering array of drips, inhalers and drugs. Every time he has visitors, which is frequently, he persuades them to get him into a wheelchair and they push him along to the lift and then out into the car park so he can have a smoke, with one of his visitors holding an umbrella over him against the snow. A nurse confided to me that he was doing "much better" now, having cut down from over 60 a day. I never got to know his name, but he waves and wheezes a "good luck".

Jim is, of course, glued to the television in the dining room and Ged is off on his wanderings, hiding from physiotherapists no doubt, so I shake Peter's frail hand and say goodbye.

"Don't you dare come back," he tells me.

I tell him he can bank on that.

It is bliss to be home again.

Alyson has removed all the ashtrays from my office and refilled the salt cellars with Lo Salt. There are two mailbags full of post — mostly books for review or entries for the Crime Writers' Association's Gold and Silver Dagger Awards, of which I am one of the judges. There are also scores of emails, most of them messages from fellow crime writers and one from Marcel Berlins, of BBC Radio 4's *Law in Action* and a fellow crime critic, which I continue to treasure:

Naturally, when I hear about a friend's illness, my mind turns to litigation. You may sue the following for negligence: the cigarette manufacturers, all makers of unhealthy food and drink, your good lady wife (for cooking and/or allowing you to consume unhealthy foods), the hospital, all nurses and doctors who saw you (except Dr Ow, who acted with consummate regard to the law), all nurses and doctors who didn't see you but should have, whoever took the decision to let you out too soon (yes, I know it was you, but please find some other sucker). Possibly the drivers taking you to and from the hospital. Also, you can sue for libel the physiotherapists who forced you to appear to be gay; your reputation has clearly suffered — all those people to whom you've boasted about your heterosexuality will now think of you as a liar and a hypocrite, a most fruitful ground of damages. I

happen to be having my annual sale of my fees —
three lawsuits for the price of four.

Yours, etc.

A leading Q.C.

I haven't been home long before the phone rings and as
I happen to be sitting next to it, I answer. A familiar
voice trills in my ear: "Darling! Thank God you can
speak! I was afraid I wouldn't be able to understand a
word you said."

It is Minette Walters, who has been keeping in touch
with Aly during my absence. Once I have assured her
that I can walk and talk unaided, she insists I take the
family down to her place in Dorset for a holiday. I
promise I will just as soon as the school terms finish.

Not long afterwards another writer friend, Mark
Timlin, calls and rather hesitantly asks if I'm OK as
he's heard bad things on the grapevine. I reassure him
with John Connolly's line that only the good die young
and with one from my books: It's better to be lucky
than good.

I decide to send a mass email to avoid having to tell
the same stories over and over again and so I spend all
of one day carefully pecking out a "Health Report" as if
it was a Royal bulletin pinned to the gates of
Buckingham Palace.

I detail all the highlights, from Connie the
nightstalker to the Gay Air Hostess exercises and send
it to just about everyone I know. The replies I receive
are heart warming and the best thing possible for my
morale. The writer Stella Duffy, herself a survivor of

cancer, suggests we meet up to swap life threatening illnesses. The agent Jane Gregory suggests I turn my Health Report into a newspaper feature, something my editor at the Birmingham Post actually does, even paying me for it. Medieval mystery supremo Paul Doherty has a Mass said for me at his local church and sends me the contents (personally augmented, I suspect) of the collection plate. George Harding, my book dealer friend, offers us the use of a cottage in Wales for a holiday and the Pakistani businessman Naseem Khawaja — whom I call "the Kashmiri wideboy" and who features as a character in several of my books — promises to drive up from Middlesex and take Aly and me out to dinner at Michel Roux's restaurant in Suffolk, which he eventually does.

I go through a period of euphoria, convinced that I have recovered and that my life is back to normal. Except, of course, I haven't and it's not.

When Aly and the kids go to school, I am left alone for the first time in several weeks. Naturally, I am confident I can cope. I remember to take the pills I was prescribed by the hospital consultant — a drug called Perindopril — and my daily aspirin.

Aspirin and stroke

Aspirin has long been known to reduce the risk of heart problems and stroke by inhibiting enzymes which make platelets (tiny particles) in the blood "sticky" (i.e. aspirin "thins the blood" to help it flow freely through the veins). A small daily dose of aspirin is almost automatically prescribed to every stroke survivor and it is thought to cut the risk of having another stroke by about 25%.

Research at Lausanne University in Switzerland (reported by the BBC in 2005) suggests that this positive effect of aspirin is very quickly lost if you stop taking it.

The Swiss research suggests that a survivor who takes aspirin and then gives up on it is three times more at risk of another stroke in the short term than a patient who has never taken it.

I go for a walk around our village, determined to start a regular exercise programme. Both my American friend Ray Daniloff and Minette Walters urge me to get a dog to accompany me on these walks. We have cats at home but they just don't seem interested in coming along. In fact they are quite dismissive when I suggest it.

There has been a lull in the winter snowstorms, but it is still cold and I feel the cold a lot more than I ever used to. I also tire easily and around 3p.m. each day I fall asleep for anything up to an hour, which is not like me at all. I decide that more exercise and fresh air is the answer and so one afternoon, to avoid the drowsiness, I decide to cut some firewood in the old milking stalls which we use as an all purpose garden shed.

I manage to saw one seasoned log into grate size pieces and by then I am dripping with sweat and more tired than ever. In the shed is an ancient fruit crate made of thin plywood, which once held apples but which we use for kindling wood. It is almost empty, so I decide to chop kindling as the easier option to sawing tree trunks.

With hindsight I can categorically *not* recommend chopping kindling with a hand axe as a good form of physiotherapy. As soon as I bend over to chop my first log, I feel unbalanced. Raising the axe above my head, I lose all my senses and start to topple backwards. Fortunately, the axe falls harmlessly to the floor. I fall backwards and sit on — and then in — the empty kindling crate, my weight and the size of my backside smashing the sides so that the damn think fits round me like a ballet dancer's tutu. I come to rest with my feet about six inches off the ground, firmly stuck by the buttocks inside the crate. I can't help laughing, it is so ridiculous, then I realise that Aly and the kids will be home soon and I don't want them to see me like this. Aly will laugh herself sick and the kids will not allow me to forget it — ever.

I know something of how a lobster must feel in a pot, but I am far less graceful in my attempts to escape, writhing from side to side until the frame of the crate eventually splinters and I get to my knees, and then my feet, with what little dignity I have left and brush the dirt and sawdust from my clothes.

So much for chopping wood. For safety's sake, I determine to stick to household chores and walks around the village. Yet even those have their dangers.

Back from work Aly asks what the hell has been going on. I have no idea what she means until she points out that every door of every cupboard in the kitchen is wide open and I realise I had assumed I had closed them *with my left hand*, but nothing had happened.

I begin to notice — or rather Aly and the kids notice — an increasing number of small things where I forget to do something, or have forgotten I already have. Forgetting to bring the milk in from the front doorstep is a favourite one, but others include forgetting where I've left my glasses, to take my daily pills, or to wear a coat when I go outside, even though the snow and ice have returned with a vengeance.

I am also incapable of staying awake beyond 3p.m. and Aly will return from work to find me slumped in a chair and assume I have been watching daytime TV.

This goes beyond a quick "power nap". Almost on the dot of 3p.m., I virtually pass out — one day I actually do fall asleep on my feet and keel over, crashing on to the living room floor — and there seems little I can do to resist. I realise I cannot hope to go back to work in this state, or drive, or do anything which requires concentration. I haven't attempted to write anything beyond an email and my reading has slowed down substantially (before the stroke I could get through the better part of five novels a week).

I have made an appointment to see my GP, Dr Milne, and I have an outpatient's appointment at the hospital with the consultant, but both are over two weeks away, so I decide to really put some effort into this exercise thing to see if I can snap out of my torpor.

We live on one of the few patches of natural heathland left in Essex and I work out that to walk around the edge of it, then down a lane through the fields until I hit the road, bringing me to Mrs Singh's newsagents, and then back along the main Cambridge road until I hit the footpath which joins the bridleway back to the heath, is about a two mile round trip. That sounds like good exercise to me and I can pick up a newspaper on the way.

And so the next morning, I embark on my trek, having wrapped up warmly as it has snowed overnight. The countryside is quite beautiful and deadly quiet with no traffic on the lanes and I manage perhaps a third of my planned circuit before I experience severe breathlessness. I am also incredibly cold, shivering violently and I know my initial brisk walking pace has slowed to a slouch. At one point along the lane, I think I am going to collapse into the snow which has drifted against the hedgerow. I am a good quarter of a mile from the nearest house and there isn't a vehicle or human being in sight.

Later on, I call this my "Captain Oates" moment, thinking I might just have wandered off into the snow never to be found. But unlike Oates in the Antarctic, who had nobler motives, I was just trying to get that morning's *Guardian*.

It is just too ridiculous, so I force myself onward and actually do make it to the newsagent's where Mrs Singh greets me with "Day off, is it?"

I don't stop to chat as I usually do but head for home and take an odd sort of comfort that now I am walking on a main road so that somebody will see me if I die of exhaustion or exposure, though whether any of the cars speeding by would actually stop if I did is a moot point.

Back home, I turn the heating up, open a tin of soup and collapse. My two mile walk has taken me two and a half hours and when Aly gets home she sees instantly that something has happened and that I have not been watching the black and white movie on Channel 4.

She analyses the situation far quicker than I could. Did you feel like this in hospital? No. Then what's different? The drugs? Exactly.

In a flash she's on the phone to the hospital and gets through to the stroke consultant's office. From the kitchen I eavesdrop on her describing my symptoms in no uncertain terms.

"Extreme lethargy . . . no energy for anything . . ."
Well, that was fair enough.
"Sensitive to the cold, which is unlike him . . ."
True. I am, after all, from Yorkshire originally.
"Shortage of breath without exertion . . ."
Absolutely.
"Unable to concentrate, short tempered . . ."
Hang on a minute.
"Severely depressed, prone to violent mood swings . . ."
Now steady on.

"The consultant will get back to you," Aly tells me and a few hours later his secretary rings. I am to stop taking the Perindopril *immediately* and report to my GP as soon as I can.

Twenty-four hours later I feel fine, much more sociable and with lots more energy. As I throw away the remaining tablets of Perindopril — which I am now convinced are responsible for all the sins on Earth — I do something I have never done before. I rescue that folded sheet of paper which comes in every packet of prescription medicines, and I actually read it.

Under the heading "Undesirable effects" (in very small print) are listed the following side effects: cough, headache, mood or sleep changes, fatigue, generalised weakness, malaise, faintness with cold sweats, dizziness, skin rashes, skin flushes or itching, taste disturbance, nausea, abdominal pain, uncommon bronchospasm, joint pain.

The leaflet assures me that such side effects are rare and usually mild, but occasional dizziness and weariness do occur with the tablets and so I should avoid driving or operating machines.

If, however, I experience swelling of the face, lips, mouth, tongue or throat, I should consult my doctor immediately.

Once again, it seems I have got off lightly, but my struggle with drugs has only just begun.

CHAPTER
SIX

Drugs, diet and depression

It is only now that I begin to realise the scale of the task ahead if I am to reclaim anything of my old life.

On the health front, I am told that my priority must be to avoid having another stroke. Because the cause of my first one was almost certainly high blood pressure (hypertension), that has to be brought under control.

It is on my increasingly frequent visits to my GP that I start to learn about blood pressure and the range of treatments for it. In hospital I had happily submitted to having my blood pressure (Bp) measured twice a day, yet not once had it occurred to me to ask why or what the results were. Now I go on a crash course to educate myself.

As my doctor explains it, there is a large family of drugs that will lower and control blood pressure and it is usually a straightforward matter of finding the one (or two or more in combination) which suits me. It is important to find the right drug — one that will work whilst not affecting my quality of life as I will be taking them for the rest of my life.

Drugs for high blood pressure

The "family" of medicines for treating high blood pressure can be subdivided into the following groups of tablets. Remember that all medicines should be prescribed by a doctor and that most drugs have two names, a drug name and a trade name, and are available in different dosages. The examples cited here are simply those which I have been prescribed.

Diuretics

Sometimes known as Water Tablets. All diuretics work by increasing the amount of salt and fluid put out by the kidneys in urine. A traditional medicine for high blood pressure, often used in combination with other drugs these days. Side effects could include: dizziness, impotence and a risk of gout. *Examples:* Bendrofluazide, Indapamide, Spironolactone with Frusemide.

Beta Blockers

Beta blockers work by reducing a particular hormone called *angiotensin II* which is produced in the kidney. The main side effect is to slow the heart rate, though this in itself is not necessarily a problem. They can, however, cause tiredness and lethargy and you may feel the cold more in extremities such as hands and feet, all of which are known as "subtle side effects" which are not serious, but may affect your quality of life. Once the medicine of first choice, beta blockers are now used less often. Examples: Atenolol, Bisoprolol.

ACE Inhibitors

ACE stands for Angiontensin Converting Enzyme and it is often the first treatment for younger patients. These too work by stopping the production of the *angiontensin ll* hormone in the kidney and are thought to be even more effective if you reduce the amount of salt in your diet. They also work well with diuretics, but many are short acting and may have to be taken more than once a day. Side effects are, theoretically, few, the most common one being a dry cough, skin rashes, sore throat and stuffed up nose. *Examples:* Perindopril.

Angiotensin Receptor Blockers (ARBs)

Also known as Angiotensin ll Antagonists. Among the latest breed of blood pressure drugs, ARBs block *the effects* of the angiotensin hormone rather than inhibiting its production. Said to have very few side effects, although dizziness and allergic reactions have been known. *Examples:* Valsartan, Candesartan, Losartan.

Calcium Channel Blockers

There are several types of Calcium channel blockers but they all work by relaxing the body's arteries (the large blood vessels), causing them to dilate which leads to a fall in blood pressure. Thought to be among the most effective drugs for patients with severely high blood pressure. Side effects can range from headaches, fatigue and nausea to swelling of the ankles, swollen gums, increased frequency of passing urine (in men) and constipation. *Examples:* Verapamil, Amlodipine.

Alpha Blockers
Alpha blockers relax the blood vessels, causing them to open wider thus reducing the resistance to the flow of blood and lowering blood pressure. They are rarely used as a first treatment, usually brought into play when other drugs have failed to control your blood pressure. Side effects can include a sudden fall in blood pressure if you stand up suddenly (known as **postural hypertension**) leading to vertigo, nausea and dizziness, also "stress incontinence" in women.

Direct Vasodilators
Nowadays only used when blood pressure is very difficult to control or when you suffer side effects from other, more modern drugs. *Examples:* Hydralazine.

Centrally Acting
Centrally acting medicines act directly on the brain to lower blood pressure and tend to be prescribed (like Direct Vasodilators) when blood pressure has proved difficult to control, and usually in combination with other drugs. Side effects can include drowsiness, nasal stuffiness and, after high doses, depression. *Examples:* Moxonidine.

Of course, finding the right drug to suit me turns out to be far from straightforward. The nurses told me in hospital that I would be taking a daily aspirin for the rest of my life and I can handle that as at least I've heard of aspirin. These other drugs are a mystery, although when *diuretics* are mentioned, I grin stupidly and say: "I've also found that five pints of lager work well enough."

Oddly enough in the 21st century, no one is quite sure *why* diuretics work to reduce blood pressure or exactly what the relationship between water retained in the body and blood pressure is. Yet encouraging you to pass more water is possibly one of the oldest known treatments.

In a fit of desperation when modern medicines seem to be failing me, I call in at a local Chinese Herbal Medical Centre, partly because a sign says that "Dr Hu" is on duty and I can't resist being treated by a Dr Who. After taking my blood pressure, and being appalled at it, Dr Hu recommends a course of herbal teas augmented with a "brew" of "special herbs". The doctor advises that I add honey to this medicinal tea as she says I will find it bitter to the taste. She is not kidding. I follow the instructions, boiling up a sachet of special herbs with a medicinal teabag and the resulting mixture is thick and jet black. Even with honey, it is like drinking battery acid from a muddy pool and I manage about two teaspoonfuls before marching out into the garden and throwing the whole lot on the compost heap. Alyson looks at the remains of the special herbs and immediately identifies them as dandelions, which in French are known as "pissenlit" or "wet the bed" — a well known diuretic.

Still, I am determined to do everything I can to get better and embark on the quest for a drug which works but does not impinge on my quality of life. It is not easy, as just about everything I try either doesn't have any effect on my blood pressure at all, or my blood pressure comes down but I react badly to the side effects.

For the first time in my life I begin to read those slips of white paper which come with most medicines. (Previously, I have only ever taken things like paracetamol or ibuprofen and then mostly for hangovers.) I discover that I can suffer side effects not thought of by the manufacturers, though the advice given with some drugs can be confusing at best. For example, one drug I tried claimed that its side effects could be both diarrhoea *and* constipation.

In the first year after my stroke, I go through at least 16 different drugs in various combinations (plus aspirin) and suffer from side effects ranging from a sore throat and mild dizziness, to violent nausea, incontinence, impotence and extreme fatigue verging on narcolepsy. I am constantly plagued by an itchy scalp (as if I have terrible dandruff, though I haven't) and I break out in acne on a scale unknown since I was a teenager. I am also increasingly convinced that my hair and beard are growing out of control and taking on the texture of barbed wire, which is quite amusing as most men my age are worrying about going bald.

Hair growth

Meeting other stroke survivors reassures me that I am not alone in these symptoms.

Women, in particular, complain about their hair becoming uncontrollable after a stroke and one particular drug, a direct vasodilator (Minoxidil), is known to increase facial hair and women are not advised to take it.

The cumulative effect of these side effects is that my self-confidence nosedives, I get frustrated with every little thing which goes wrong, I snap irritably at my family, I rarely go out (even though I have got back to driving), I avoid talking on the telephone as my throat dries up and my voice simply cuts out, and I become more and more depressed. The depression isn't helped by practical concerns such as not having a job or a regular source of income and I am conscious that our savings are dwindling fast.

One of the cruellest knocks comes when my publisher of the last five years decides to drop me from their list, although they don't actually tell me this. I have to discover the fact by reading their half yearly catalogue of forthcoming titles and realising I am not in it.

Depression

The most common, and least quantified, consequence of stroke is **depression**, which I have seen rather primly described as "known to be associated with a deterioration in the quality of life".

A detailed study of 156 first time stroke survivors in Finland found clinical depression diagnosed *in over half of them* (53%) at three months post-stroke. A year on and 42%

were still suffering depression and "sexual impairment" was thought to be a key factor.

M-L Kauhanen, *Quality of Life After Stroke*, *University of Oulu, 2000.*

During those darkest days, about six months post-stroke, I decide to declutter my life, or at least thin out my collection of crime novels, reasoning, rather morbidly, that it will save Alyson the trouble of getting rid of them after I've gone.

I have something like 4,000 crime novels, amassed over 20 years as a reader, then author, then as a reviewer. Many are signed by fellow crime writers and friends and therefore valuable only to me, but a lot of titles are long out of print and would be of interest to a dedicated crime fiction buff. Using the internet I begin to contact specialist dealers and I email friends to see if there is anything in my collection they would like in theirs.

This exercise doesn't actually get me very far, and I end up with several boxes of almost new paperbacks which I decide to give to the local charity shops. Then I remember that the hospital deals in books for patients and visitors — I'd bought several there myself — and decide to take them a load.

I find that the Stroke Unit, as it is now officially called, has moved out of Birch Ward into ground floor accommodation and it does indeed have a small library/book stall for patients. Whilst I am dropping off a box of books, one of the nurses (it might even have

106

been Sally, my "dedicated nurse") recognises me and, naturally, asks how I am.

I tell her that I am actually feeling worse now than when I had the stroke and I wouldn't mind the lousy side effects of the drugs if they actually worked, but nothing seems to and my blood pressure remains stubbornly high. She tells me she read about a new medicine, being developed in Japan, on the internet and whilst she's telling me this, she asks if I've contacted the Blood Pressure Association.

Of course I had not, as I'd never heard of it before now, but as soon as I get home I find their website (**www.bpassoc.org.uk**) and learn more about blood pressure in half an hour than I had ever known in my life. I request some of their publications, leave questions on their helpline facility and even apply to join the association.

I am still a member and help out in publicity campaigns where I can. I found the quality and helpfulness of their advice and printed material to be second to none and I will be ever grateful to them for the fact that they recommended that I join Different Strokes, of which I had not heard until then.

In hospital I had been encouraged to read some of the (usually excellent) pamphlets published by the Stroke Association, but I had not been contacted by them or urged to join a local stroke club since my discharge. In truth, there was little enthusiasm on my part as my impression of stroke clubs was that they were *for old people* and, in the words of one nurse who advised against me visiting one, "you're not ready for bingo and basket weaving just yet".

This sounds terribly dismissive of the great social good done by hundreds of stroke clubs and thousands of volunteers, day in day out, and it is certainly not meant to be. It is just that, at 50, and physically more recovered than many stroke victims, they were not for me. I was greedy to have some of my former life back, and terrified of the thought that I might not.

Different Strokes, I discovered, is a national charity aimed at supporting the younger stroke survivor, notionally the under 55s. Their "welcome pack" of information was very welcome indeed and I am still, to this day, amazed and appalled that hospital Stroke Units do not automatically recommend Different Strokes to younger stroke survivors. But best of all was their website, though not, you might think, for the most noble of reasons.

The Different Strokes website is www.differentstrokes.co.uk but be warned if you use a search engine: "different strokes" is also a website address for lesbian, gay, bisexual and transgender swimming clubs in San Diego and Calgary, Canada.

The DS website has one priceless component and that is the section called "Survivors' Stories" where members are actively encouraged to relate their experiences of having a stroke. Finding these personal stories was a cathartic experience for me. As I read them, I realised that *I was not alone*. Others of my age, many who were younger, had suffered similar problems not just with the stroke itself, but with medication and rehabilitation in general.

I was so relieved that *someone else was suffering too*.

More importantly, other stroke survivors *were recovering and getting back to work, back into relationships and back to their lives*. There was hope here. These were people who had not given up on hope. I joined, and a year later found myself working part time as their Regional Coordinator for East Anglia.

My discovering Different Strokes and the Blood Pressure Association was, I am convinced now, a turning point in my recovery. I was still a long way from finding medication which I could live with and still struggling to keep fit (or at least awake) and fighting off bouts of depression, which invariably lead to verbal bust ups with my wife and inexcusable temper tantrums usually involving the children. I had put on about 20 pounds in weight after giving up smoking, I was unemployed for the first time ever and, for the first time in 15 years, I did not have a publisher urging me to write a new book.

Different Strokes had shown me that stroke victims could reclaim their lives, even if it wasn't exactly the life they had before. The BPA taught me about my own personal enemy, blood pressure, and, as in any war situation, good intelligence is vital. I was determined to start to fight back — to launch a counter-attack — and the weapon I chose was to finish the novel I had been writing when so rudely interrupted by the stroke.

The vocabulary of strokes

The term "stroke victim" is a contentious one in some circles. Some prefer "stroke survivor" (a "victim" being a non-survivor) as being more politically correct, but by far the majority of survivors I have met refer to themselves as "victims" on the grounds that they never went looking for a stroke in the first place.

The book in question is, unusually for me, an historical novel rather than comic crime fiction and, when I had my stroke, I had completed some 45,000 words out of a projected 140,000 under the working title *The Real, True Story of Boudica (Probably)*. It is set in Britain at the time of Queen Boudica's revolt against the occupying legions of Rome and will be thoroughly based on my experiences as an archaeologist after three years digging Romano-British sites in East Anglia, including several areas actually destroyed in the rebellion.

I had got the idea whilst digging on a site in Colchester which was visited by a news crew from Anglia TV. The cameraman somehow recognised me as a crime writer and I was interviewed whilst digging a particularly boring piece of the "Boudican destruction horizon" — a layer of compressed black ash which is just about all that is left of the capital of Roman Britain circa 60AD.

In about 30 seconds I tried to get across some of the drama of the revolt of Boudica (the Queen formerly known as "Boadicea") and the presenter interviewing me said that the story sounded as "exciting as one of your thriller plots." On reflection, it's probably *better*! That night I began my detailed research and began writing in the Autumn of 2002, having persuaded Colin Dexter (a Classics master until he turned his hand to creating Inspector Morse) to help with translations into and out of Latin.

But then came the stroke. Fortunately most of my research was complete, but picking up where I left off was a daunting task. I had to get to grips again with about 30 characters, the landscape, tribes and religions of Iron Age Britain, the politics and economics of the Roman Empire under Nero, the tactics and weaponry of the Roman Army and the plot I had devised to get over the many gaps in the historical record. All this in a manuscript I had not looked at for about five months.

I settle down to a thorough read through and I impress myself with the speed with which I pick up the thread, making copious notes in pencil about what needs to be done to finish the thing. Getting back to actually writing is not going to be as straightforward though, not with my left hand and arm still restricted to fairly clumsy, large movements with little "fine motor" control.

For a long time post-stroke, I was unable to hold things in both hands without the left hand starting to shake. Trying to hold a mug of tea in each hand was a recipe for disaster, as was attempting to carry two pints of beer in a pub. This gave me a good excuse to stop buying drinks for other people for about two years. Today the condition is hardly noticeable, which just goes to show that improvement after stroke can happen even if it seems to take an age.

Every attempt to sit at the computer keyboard and write ends in total frustration, anger and some ripe swear words, not to mention the overwhelming desire to dash out and buy cigarettes. As long as my left hand has a mind of its own, I'm getting nowhere, so I revert to pen and paper, working on the dining room table, but it just doesn't feel right. I have, after all, been working with the printed word since university days and still have two typewriters in reasonable working order.

With nothing to lose, I drag a 40 year old German portable out of the garden shed and spray the mechanism with oil until all the keys start to move. I even find, through Yellow Pages, one of the last remaining independent stationers still in business in Colchester and, amazingly in these computer dominated days, he still sells typewriter *ribbons*, although he only has three left in stock.

Alyson comes home from work to find me happily bashing away at the typewriter keys and the floor covered with screwed up balls of paper. For the first couple of days I simply concentrate on making my left hand work on the keyboard, remembering the days when I could achieve a fair speed touch-typing — certainly faster than many a secretary I've worked with.

Very quickly, and wisely, I stop bothering with content or accuracy. In fact for three days I am typing absolute gibberish and then I begin to type up some of my handwritten notes for the Boudica book. My left hand responds well. It still feels strangely numb and stiff but at least it doesn't have a mind of its own. After three weeks I take a deep breath and move back on to the computer, first making several copies of the manuscript to date in case I delete the lot in my enthusiasm.

It is now that another problem rears its ugly head. Every morning I sit there facing a blank screen and try to pick up the story where I left it. I know what has to be done; I know how the characters develop; I know how it all ends (badly — for Boudica); but my brain simply does not want to engage first gear and let me get started. I play computer games such as Free Cell and Hearts, surf the internet, send dozens of emails — anything to avoid getting down to writing. It is as if I am still half asleep and simply cannot get going mentally and numerous cups of strong coffee don't help.

I convince myself that the one thing missing from my normal writing routine, now that my left hand is behaving, is the cigarette I would automatically light up as I sat down at a keyboard.

By this stage, I was sure I had kicked the smoking habit. I had not had a cigarette since the day I was admitted to hospital and had used nicotine patches (which can be obtained on prescription) to ward off the worst of the withdrawal cravings.

On a routine visit to my GP that week, I mentioned that I was having problems concentrating and "getting my brain in gear" in the mornings. Without any promptings about cigarettes, he said: "It's the nicotine you're missing. Your brain liked it and got used to it, and now it's gone."

I make the link that whilst *smoking* was obviously bad for me, bunging up arteries over the years so that my blood pressure increased, the nicotine itself was the stimulant I had come to rely on to kick start my brain and everything I read seemed to suggest that nicotine itself would not increase my blood pressure in the long run.

And so, tentatively, I try the various proprietary brands of nicotine chewing gum, quickly discovering that "normal" strength (4 mg nicotine) make me feel physically sick, (as do nicotine patches nowadays), but the low strength variety (2 mg nicotine) do have the desired effect. My concentration improves and I begin to write again, but limiting myself to no more than three pieces of the gum in a day when I need to concentrate. (The manufacturers estimate that most people chew 10 pieces a day.)

Instead of dreading a morning staring blankly at the computer, I begin to make serious inroads into the novel, adding almost 100,000 words over the next 10 months, determined not to give up, having invested so much time and emotion in the damned thing. It is eventually published as *Boudica and the Lost Roman* on my 53rd birthday in 2005.

Giving up smoking

I do NOT recommend my experience with nicotine to anyone, but that is what worked for me. If smoking helped to cause my stroke, it did so via the physical ingestion of smoke rather than a mental dependence on the drug nicotine — or so I convince myself. The majority of younger stroke survivors I have met over the last three years never did smoke, and most of the ones who did managed to quit with the help of nicotine patches.

Now back to writing again, I decide to try and optimise my situation.

I am taking my medication and suffering only minor, tolerable, side effects (not realising that the drugs are having absolutely no effect on my blood pressure at this point). I have got my arm and hand working again so that I can type and I am managing to concentrate on writing. The next things to do are concentrate on diet and exercise.

Diet and hypertension

Most health diets recommend foods rich in **potassium** and **magnesium** to help keep blood pressure under control. Potassium rich foods include avocados, bananas, grapefruit, melons, oranges, broccoli and peas. Magnesium rich foods include nuts, rice, bananas (again), potatoes, wheat germ and lima beans.

The American crime writer Walter Satterthwait is keen to recommend garlic (which I have always liked) to me. It is said to lower blood pressure by 5–10% (which makes me wonder what my Bp would have been if I had never eaten it), to be able to lower cholesterol, promote blood circulation and discourage the formation of blood clots.

In folklore, of course, garlic's association with the blood supply is very important, in that it wards off vampires. In Roman times it was used as a treatment for madness but also taken, boiled in wine, with fresh coriander as an aphrodisiac.

I have always had a good diet, just too much of it, and I was always guilty of using too much salt, that I admit. Well, the salt has now gone and, probably because I no longer smoke, I don't miss it very much. I can taste food better and if needed, I can substitute pepper (black, white and cayenne). We never ate very much processed food, which forms the main source of salt in many people's diets, and I was never one of those fair weather pub goers who couldn't have a night down the local without two packets of crisps and some dry roasted peanuts.

All the available advice tells me to eat more fruit, which is not a problem. In fact I quickly slip into the habit of substituting an apple when I would normally have taken a cigarette break and having oranges, pineapples, melons or bananas as desserts. I have absolutely no problem eating the recommended five fruits a day, I begin to lose weight and, most noticeably, I am far less prone to catching colds.

Cholesterol

In many respects, my situation is easy to handle as it is not complicated by problems with **cholesterol**, about which much is said but probably little is understood, including by me. At the time of my stroke, my cholesterol level was 4.2 and I was told that this was a good thing. But where it is a problem, doctors will often prescribe **statins**, cholesterol lowering drugs (such as Atorvastatin). There are two types of cholesterol: low density lipoproteins, often referred to as **LDLs** or **bad** cholesterol, and high density lipoproteins, or **HDLs**, the **good** cholesterol. The higher the HDLs are as a proportion of the total cholesterol in the body, the better. Most cholesterol in the blood is produced naturally by the body but the amount of dietary cholesterol eaten (in full fat dairy products and animal fats, for instance) can affect overall levels.

A simple blood test will indicate if you have a problem with your cholesterol level and your doctor will advise on your diet and the use of statins. Always take proper medical advice and do not attempt to buy statins, which can have numerous side effects, or any other drugs for that matter, over the internet.

I realise that I have not been to a pub for months, although no one has ever said I should give up alcohol. My reluctance has been partly self-conscious — a fear of appearing clumsy and awkward in a busy public place — and partly a genuine fear that I would not be able to resist the temptation to smoke again, as I had always smoked in pubs. I decide to tackle the problem head on and enlist two friends to act as bodyguards. They have orders not to let me smoke no matter how hard I beg or how loud I cry and, despite the fact that one of them smokes a big cigar in front of me, I make it through a very pleasant evening and am quite proud of myself.

But if I am serious about my diet and healthy eating regime, I must put my beer drinking days behind me and I switch to drinking wine, particularly red wine which I dilute half and half with water.

Having mastered nicotine and come to a sensible accommodation with alcohol, I thought I had the potentially dangerous things sorted out. I was unaware that the most dangerous thing I was to do was exercise.

Now, to be fair, no one had ever told me to go swimming, but then again, no one had told me not to. Swimming had been the one form of exercise (the only one) I had actually enjoyed; it was something we could do as a family and I knew it was good for you. My wife and eldest daughter were both excellent swimmers, far stronger than I, and our two youngest had been confident in the water from the age of six or seven.

So, during a school half-term, we all visit the local Leisure Centre and while the kids jump into the Olympic sized pool, I lower myself in rather gingerly, but confident that this is going to do me good. Already the rest of the family is down the other end of the pool and I set off at a sedate pace to swim to them.

I realise that I can't swim any more when I'm about six feet under the surface *and going down* at the deep end of the pool. It dawns on me, almost in slow motion, that I have absolutely no power in my left arm or left leg and they are acting like dead weights in the water even though they are making all the right movements. The result is that I do a slow anti-clockwise roll and head for the bottom of the pool, rather like a shot porpoise. The kids, who have spotted me by now, think this is some sort of game and they swim underwater alongside me, grinning and gesticulating happily in response to my frantic waving. I want to shout out that *I'm not waving, I'm drowning!*

I can clearly see the bottom of the pool now and am having trouble holding my breath. Surely someone must realise I'm in trouble. Fortunately, Alyson has seen me disappear under the water and not reappear and has shot across the pool to grab me by the arm and pull me, gasping, to the surface.

Hanging on to the side of the pool I realise that all this has happened right in front of the pool's totally unconcerned lifeguard, who is perched on one of those ladder chairs which tennis umpires use. From up there, looking down on the surface of the pool, he hadn't realised that I was heading down, rather than along, as from the top I looked to be making all the correct swimming movements.

Alyson says not to worry and just to float around for a bit until I get my confidence back. Everyone can float, can't they? I can't; not any more.

I can manage about 10 seconds on my back and then I very slowly roll to my left and start to sink. Alyson immediately thinks I'm acting up but I am powerless to stop myself. After going under for the tenth time, I give up and clamber out of the pool, having decided to stick to walking.

I realise why I had never done much exercise in the past — it's bloody dangerous!

It is over a year before I go back in the water. American friends take us to the beautiful Outer Banks coastline of North Carolina and there the conditions are perfect for splashing in the Atlantic surf. Our host, Joe Maron, is a laconic New Yorker who watches from the beach while the family plunges in the waves. Summoning up all my courage I decide to join them. After all, I needn't go out of my depth and I can always put my feet down if I'm in trouble. I convince myself I'll be fine as I'll only be in about three feet of water. Yes, I'm going to do it! I pull off my shirt and take one confident step towards the ocean. It is at precisely that moment that Joe, a former US Navy man, says philosophically: "Well, I guess the sharks don't usually come this close inshore."

I think what the hell, I'll probably drown before the sharks get here, and take the plunge. Later that week, after several more dips in the sea, I manage an entire width in a swimming pool without having to send up a distress flare. It's only a width, not a length, but it's a start.

CHAPTER
SEVEN

The numbers game

In my first year as a stroke survivor, I try to be the perfect patient. I change my lifestyle as and when instructed, I try to exercise, I take my medication without fail and I try to educate myself about stroke and hypertension on the basis that knowledge is power and I ought to know my enemy if I am going to beat him.

Yet despite my best efforts, and the patience and perseverance of my GP, my blood pressure (Bp) remains stubbornly high.

I never do find out what my Bp readings were in the hospital (I never bothered to ask) but in the first 10 months post-stroke, my blood pressure is taken once a fortnight in my doctor's surgery. Of those 20 readings, which my doctor presents me with in the form of a bar chart, not one came close to my "healthy" target of 140/80. The average was probably 170/95, though on one spectacular occasion it shot up to 205/82 and on another it plummeted down to 132/80.

My all time record to date is 220/108.

There is an old wives' tale that your ideal blood pressure should be 100 + your age.

If that was the case, then I had my 120th birthday last year, yet this year I was 36 again.

Not only was my blood pressure high, it was out of control and this was a period when I was trying a new drug virtually every month. Not only were they not working, they were producing side effects ranging from mildly irritating and embarrassing skin rashes to intensely depressing sexual impotence, which is often a by-product of stroke itself, but in my case did not set in until seven months post-stroke and was, I think, directly attributable to the blood pressure medicines.

Bp readings — those two little (or not so little in my case) numbers — come to dominate, if not my life, then my recovery.

I think I have done just about everything I can. I have improved my diet, lost weight, started taking exercise (walking not swimming!), kept my brain busy by getting back to writing my historical novel and tried not to get too depressed about the lack of a sex life and no regular job or prospect of one. I actually feel guilty about taking up time in my doctor's surgery on what seems likely to become a fruitless quest to get those all important numbers to come down.

My GP, though, is not prepared to give up on me and suggests that I invest in a Bp monitoring machine so I can take readings at home. He warns me, though, not to become obsessed with them and he explains what is known as the "white coat effect" — an allowance of about 10 mmHg (degrees of mercury) when your blood pressure is taken by a doctor or a

122

nurse in a medical setting is made to counter the stress of the situation. Taking my own readings at home in a familiar environment may well give a truer (lower) set of readings. This is comforting in one respect, but worrying in another in that it shows what a fairly blunt instrument blood pressure is and there are no guarantees in this area. I didn't know I had high blood pressure until I had a stroke. Getting my Bp down can't guarantee I won't have another one, but it is the only course of action I have if I am to give myself a fighting chance of avoiding the really bad bullet.

Personal blood pressure monitors

At the time I started shopping around for a battery operated "fuzzy logic" Blood Pressure Monitor, I could not find a single pharmacy which stocked one, although they all offered to order one if I knew what I wanted. My doctor recommended the arm cuff type (as in hospitals) rather than the wristband type, and I found two manufacturers quite easily through the internet: P.M.S. Instruments of Maidenhead and Seinex Electronics of Belfast. Both offered machines in the £50-£70 range and I ended up ordering mine through my local Sainsbury's pharmacy so I got the Nectar points as well.

My personal monitor is easy to use and I begin to keep charts of daily readings of my Bp along with notes of which drugs I'm on at the time, any side effects and how much exercise I'm doing. I note with amusement that, in the instruction book with my monitor, they give a chart showing Bp readings taken at five minute intervals throughout the day. The readings must be for a young, fit person as they average out at around 120/55, way lower than anything I've ever recorded.

There is one exception, though. At just before midnight, the example's Bp shoots up to 170/85. That's more like it; that's a reading I'm more familiar with; I'm always clocking in at that level.

It is only then that I notice a footnote to the chart which explains Bp high at midnight as being due to sexual intercourse. My respect for the patient who took the readings knows no bounds. Imagine having the presence of mind to strap on a blood pressure monitor in the middle of . . . .

As I begin to self-monitor my Bp, I am trying a new regime of drugs: an ARB (Angiotensin Receptor Blocker) called Candesartan, in conjunction with a diuretic called Indapamide and, of course, aspirin. It is a year since the stroke and this is, I think, the 18th combination of drugs I have been prescribed.

At first, I am quite excited about the results. I am recording Bps of between 150/85 and 160/92, which is still worryingly high, but a distinct improvement for me. More to the point, the fluctuation seems to be less. The only problem is that the side effects are kicking in worse than ever.

I feel permanently nauseous and lethargic; I cannot sleep at nights, but keep flaking out in the middle of the day. My face explodes with acne and my scalp itches intolerably. I am showering twice a day yet still feel as if my skin is oozing grease from every pore. In such an unattractive physical state, it hardly seems to matter whether I'm impotent or not. I get depressed, stop writing and seem to be permanently picking fights with my family.

It is what Alyson called my "supersensitive stage" when she never knew what to say to me because she was unsure how I would take it. In effect I was suffering massive mood swings, though of course I was not aware of this at the time, and having to live with and care for someone with those symptoms puts a huge strain on any relationship.

During one particularly bad bout of depression, I decide to stop taking the drugs (except for aspirin) altogether. Almost immediately I cheer up, sleep better and the acne disappears. I almost feel human again and this confirms what I have read in many places, that the incidence of hypertension patients giving up on their medication is high, because the side effects don't seem worth the cure.

I am starting to agree with them, but then, after a drug free week, I take my blood pressure and am scared to discover it has shot up to 174/110. I phone for an appointment at my doctor's surgery immediately.

The diuretic is dropped from my drugs' menu and replaced with a direct vasodilator drug, Hydralazine, which is regarded as a bit of an old fashioned remedy these days.

Hydralazine

According to the Blood Pressure Association: "Hydralazine as a medication for high blood pressure is not commonly used in the UK and is usually only given to people who have very high blood pressure, have tried other medicines first and who are still unable to lower their blood pressure" — a pretty fair summary of my situation.

But over the next two months, the results, on paper, are encouraging as my Bp starts to level out at around 139/84, the lowest readings I have managed in nearly two years and very close to my target of 140/80.

My doctor, though, is still not happy as the side effects — skin irritation, fatigue, disturbed sleeping patterns, impotence, mood swings and depression — are still as strong as ever.

Come a new year and the second anniversary of my stroke, he suggests fine tuning the dosage of the drugs and these seemingly insignificantly small changes in the strength of the tablets do make a difference. I begin to record readings of 140 *or less* over 80 as a matter of routine, and the side effects are definitely on the wane.

I cannot say I have beaten my blood pressure problem but it appears that I might, just might, have started to tame it.

HYPERtension and HYPOtension

There is an absolute irony about hypertension worthy of the novel "Catch 22". The higher your blood pressure, the more you worry about it, especially if, as in my case, it could lead to another stroke (and I might not be so lucky next time).

But if weight loss, better diet, giving up smoking, exercise and the drugs actually work, your blood pressure can fall suddenly and dramatically (a condition called, confusingly, hypotension rather than hypertension). If that happens, you actually feel pretty terrible and begin to wonder whether lowering your Bp is actually doing you any good.

I can see how easy it would be to become obsessed with knowing and trying to understand those all-important Bp readings, but over a third of the population of the UK are thought to have high blood pressure. Most of them, like me before my stroke, just don't know it.

In the grand scale of things, it probably doesn't matter in the slightest that I know that my Bp in April 2003 was 182/93, in April 2004 was 152/85 and in April 2005 was 144/82, but the fact that the trend is downwards is a great comfort to me. As is the very fact that I *know* something about my condition. I don't feel quite so helpless any more.

I am frequently amazed — and horrified — to meet stroke survivors who *have no idea* what their blood pressure is *or should be*. Of all people, they have no real excuse for not knowing. Like me, they have had a possible final warning that they should take an interest in what is going on in their bodies.

There are indications though that awareness levels are rising.

In shopping precincts, supermarkets, pharmacies and doctors' surgeries, one week every September is usually dedicated Blood Pressure Testing Week as part of the national "Know Your Numbers" campaign. In 2004, over 200,000 people were tested at more than 2,000 "pressure stations" throughout the country and for the first time in the campaign, there were more men than women involved.

There is a growing acceptance that eating more fruit and vegetables and less processed food is better for you, highlighted by the ongoing public debate about school dinners and (hopefully) hospital catering. Not only is it healthier in general, but it can quite specifically reduce the risk of hypertension, stroke and even heart attacks and certain forms of cancer.

It was the World Health Organisation (WHO) back in 1990 which identified that a daily consumption of around 400 grams of fruits and vegetables — about five portions — may help protect against heart disease and some cancers. Thus the "5 A Day" message was born, though recent thinking is that "5 to 9 (portions) A Day" would be an even better target to aim at. Today, there are labels referring to "part of your five-a-day portions" on fruit and vegetables in all major supermarkets as well as publicity campaigns in schools and doctors' surgeries, and hopefully the message will get through, though it is still probably true that, as a nation, Britain falls short of eating *three* portions a day, let alone five.

Fruit and veg and blood pressure

Eating more fruit and vegetables is important and something we all tell our children to do even if we don't follow our own advice. It is actually seriously good advice for anyone with high blood pressure.

Fruit and vegetables are our main source of **potassium**, which has a blood pressure *lowering* effect, as opposed to **sodium** which puts up your blood pressure (hence the advice to cut down on salt).

Some studies are said to have shown that increasing the fruit and vegetables in your diet from two to seven portions a day can result in a lowering of systolic Bp by around 7 mmHG.

(For example; from 150/85 to 143/85.)

The only caveat to a healthier, fruitier diet is if you have been prescribed certain calcium channel blockers or statins (to reduce cholesterol) as part of your medication. Your doctor will tell you to avoid drinking grapefruit juice as it contains elements which will react badly with the drugs. It's only grapefruit juice; other fruit juices are not a problem.

I never ever thought I would become an ambassador for healthy living having spent a fair proportion of my life in London: smoking, eating expense account lunches, drinking too much and never walking where I could take a taxi.

I'm still a long way from being the ideal role model, but I find myself increasingly intolerant of stroke survivors who refuse to make changes to their lifestyles after they have had what could, for all of us, be their first and also final warning.

I have met survivors of my age or younger, who have had three strokes and still won't quit smoking or make any changes to their diet. (Though the majority of younger stroke survivors I have come across were never smokers.)

I know it is difficult to give up. Hardly a day goes by when I don't (still) fancy a cigarette and I can't say I feel a whole lot healthier because I have given up smoking, but I am an awful lot healthier than if I had had another stroke.

If anything, the excuses people give for not changing their diet are more elaborate than for not giving up smoking. They "don't like the taste of fruit". (All fruit?) "Fruit is so boring" (!) "Fruit is too difficult to eat" (?) "It takes too long to peel". (How busy a life do you have?) "Fruit is too expensive". (So are cigarettes and funerals.)

I have even met one stroke survivor who is convinced that eating fruit was the cause of her high blood pressure.

Today there is a huge amount of publicity and promotional material about healthy eating, in surgeries, health centres, community centres, libraries, schools, supermarkets, newspapers and magazines. There is virtually no excuse for not adopting a healthier diet when the alternative could be so awful.

No one can give any guarantees of course, but eating a banana, a couple of apples and a salad a day and drinking orange juice instead of sweet fizzy drinks seems an incredibly small price to pay if it helps (even minutely) to avoid another stroke.

The level of public information on stroke and hypertension is also increasing dramatically. At a guess, I would say there are at least three times as many websites on the internet dealing with the subjects as there were in 2003 when I started my first tentative searches.

Much of the information is scientific and medical research which is difficult for the lay person to follow, even if they haven't had a stroke, but it is reassuring that so much effort seems to be being made in the field of stroke treatment and in medications for hypertension. If nothing else, the more stroke is talked about, the more it is demystified. For far too long stroke has been the illness no one really liked to talk about and my experiences in recent years have often reminded me of my childhood in Yorkshire where cancer was the "demon disease" only spoken of in hushed terms as if it was something to be ashamed of.

Not long ago, I was lectured over the phone by a woman who worked for a national medical charity, who took me to task for just using the word "stroke".

"We refer to the condition as CVA (cerebrovascular accident). We no longer use the word "stroke" because of its *stigmatic* qualities," she told me in no uncertain terms.

Of course, she couldn't have known she was talking to a survivor, let alone one who believes that the way to destigmatise something is to understand it, not just change its name.

CHAPTER
EIGHT

Picking up threads

So just how much of your old life can you reclaim after a stroke? When you find the answer to the "how long is a piece of string?" question, you'll have answered that one as well.

It depends, of course, on the severity of the stroke. Mine was a right sided blood clot (which then cleared). A bleed on the left side of the brain would have been far more serious.

In my case, I was lucky enough to experience a good chunk of recovery fairly rapidly. Despite falling over a lot, I was able to walk (albeit sometimes with the aid of a passing nurse) within a week. For many survivors, it takes much longer, after months of extensive physiotherapy. Sometimes, it does not happen at all.

In hospital I also recovered the power of speech, at least enough to be understood (and enough to complain about the food), and the basic motor function of my left arm, even if I could not control it very well. The finer movements of my left hand came back after weeks of bashing at a portable typewriter, a method of physiotherapy I would recommend to anyone who has typed or used a computer keyboard before.

So, a complete physical recovery? Far from it, even though I am repeatedly, and annoyingly, being told: *you don't look as if you've had a stroke.*

My sense of balance never did recover fully and I still casually walk into the left hand sides of door frames unless I'm concentrating. I can walk, and try to keep to my exercise regime of two miles a day, but I doubt if I could run more than 20 yards even if my life depended upon it. Nor do I trust myself any more to ride a bicycle and it will be a long time before I feel totally confident in a swimming pool.

Because of my ongoing battle with hypertension — I will never "recover" I can only hope to control it — the medication I have to take is having, if anything, a more physically debilitating effect than the stroke itself actually did.

Worst of all is the lethargy, the total, draining feeling of fatigue after fairly minimal physical exertion, best described, I think, as simply a lack of energy.

I have come to the conclusion that my body actually *likes* high blood pressure, for I seem to have much more energy when my Bp readings go into the danger zone of over 160/90. I also know, without measuring it, when my Bp has fallen to "acceptable levels" of less than 140/80, because I feel terrible (And I have a desperate craving for a cigarette, although my family tells me that's my overactive imagination).

The other side effects of blood pressure medicines (at least on me), from acne and impotence to the itchy scalp, can all be treated with other medications. Although few doctors like to prescribe one drug to counter the effects of another, they do take account of a patient's overall quality of life.

So *physically*, I'm probably back to 85–90% of my former self and there are relatively few things I cannot actually do, although I do admit to being far more nervous of heights, ladders and open staircases than I ever was.

Something I discovered in an Iron Age hill fort in Dorset. About three months after the stroke, on holiday near Dorchester I insisted on visiting Maiden Castle, a massive and very impressive fortress where Ancient Brits tried to defy the invading Romans (but failed completely). Having successfully walked up the long approach and across the entire length of the thing, the obvious way back to the car park was via a staircase cut into the side of one of the huge defensive ditches: a flight of stairs about 20 inches wide and going down almost forever, it seemed, with no banister to hang on to.

Somehow, with gritted teeth and the help of the kids, I made it down. The alternative — an archaeologist unable to get out of one of our most important archaeological sites — would have been too embarrassing to contemplate.

There are still, however, any number of small things which physically prove difficult. I am extremely clumsy — my wife would say "no change there then" —

especially when trying to carry anything which involves both hands and arms.

Plastic bags in supermarkets still drive me to distraction, as they did my fellow survivor Brian, simply trying to get the damn things open, although I'm glad to say this is not just a problem for stroke survivors. So many people have problems with them that most Coop stores (and many Tescos) now encourage their staff to flick open bags in anticipation of customers at the checkout. If only more retail staff thought about the way they gave change, that would be a help too.

Handling loose change

On my first shopping trip post-stroke, a very nice checkout girl carefully put into my hand a receipt, then a £5 note and then, on top of that, about £2.80p worth of coins.

There was no way I could sort the change, the £5 note and the receipt, with a shopping bag in one hand, without blocking the queue at the till and it would have been so much easier if she had put them down rather than in my hand, as was obviously company policy. Embarrassed by this on several occasions since, I now always go into a shop with the right hand pocket of my jacket deliberately empty. Receipt, notes, coins, whatever I'm given, goes straight in there unsorted until I get out of the shop, or home.

For many survivors, especially men, the biggest concern is when they will be able to drive again (if they can at all) as being mobile equals independence and independence becomes synonymous with life before the stroke.

I believe things are much more strict than they were in early 2003 when I was "advised" by hospital staff that I would have to give up driving for a month at least. Nobody checked and nobody sent the police round to confiscate my car keys. I was, in a way, put on my honour not to drive.

In fact, it was the last thing I felt like doing and, as I had no job to go to and my wife insisted she could do the school run and get to her job on time, it was one problem less to worry about.

I did, I think, all the right things. I rang the Driver and Vehicle Licensing Centre/Authority (DVLC or DVLA) in Swansea and eventually, after about four days (TIP: Don't ring them at the end of a calendar month when lots of drivers are trying to renew documents, something the hero of my crime novels would have known, but I forgot) found somebody to speak to who promised to send me the appropriate forms. These basically gave the DVLA permission to check with my doctor that I would be fit to drive after a month (which seemed to be the accepted period you should not attempt to drive for).

I even rang my insurance company to tell them I would not be driving for a month for medical reasons. I was not asked anything about my state of health, but I was asked repeatedly if I was cancelling my policy. I insisted I was not, merely "not using it" for a month and when I said I did not expect any sort of rebate or refund, the tone of the Call Centre lady became instantly more friendly and she said that was fine, she would make a note of it and I was to have a nice day.

About six weeks after leaving hospital, I very gingerly ran the car up and down the unmade lane (i.e. not a proper road) near our house for about two days before I felt confident enough to try driving in traffic. This I only did after a visit to my optician (I wear glasses for driving, going to the cinema or theatre and playing darts) just to check everything was as it should be, and asking my doctor if he saw any reason why I should not drive.

I know (now) that the DVLA had not got around to contacting my doctor or running any checks on me by then, because of a logjam in the system, but at the time it never occurred to me. In fact it was in July 2003 — over five months after I had left hospital and over three months since I had started driving again — that I received a letter from the DVLA stating "Enquiry indicates that you are able to satisfy the medical standards of fitness to drive relating to neurological illness. Therefore, driving may continue without the need for routine medical review of the licence."

This post-dated approval, of course, wasn't worth the paper it was printed on, as if the DVLA ever did bother to ask my doctor, it was months after I had got back on the road.

I did so very nervously at first, and avoided driving at night for about six months. The main problems I had all involved forgetting to do things I once did automatically. For example, stopping at a junction and forgetting to change gear so I would find myself trying to set off again in second or third gear. Forgetting to indicate was another one, also indicating left and then forgetting to turn left. This I realised was more serious and probably dangerous and so I took to repeating the mantra they used to teach you for your driving test: "mirror, signal, manoeuvre", saying it aloud when I was alone in the car, until it finally sank in and became (relearned) second nature. Nowadays my most common problem is forgetting to undo my seat belt before trying to get out of a car after I have parked, though I suppose that is preferable to forgetting to put it on in the first place.

Driving after a stroke

It is possible to drive again even if the stroke has left the survivor with a severe physical disability. Cars can be adapted with the latest ingenious devices, putting all the main controls on an electronic "magic box" on the steering wheel.

There are 17 Mobility Centres dotted around the country, which adapt cars, assess driving abilities and even give driving tests. [The UK Forum of Mobility Centres website is **www.mobility-centres.org.uk**]

The ability to drive again — to be mobile and independent — means so much to stroke survivors, it is impossible to quantify. For some it is a positive incentive to work towards recovery. For others who cannot recover sufficiently and who may have their driving licences taken away, it can be heartbreaking.

I know of one survivor who returned to driving five years post-stroke then, after two years of independent mobility, had her licence revoked. A year later she is back on the road with a new car, suitably adapted so that she can control everything from the steering wheel. A fellow survivor of Birch Ward, who had a stroke about a month before mine, actually got his Heavy Goods Vehicle licence back and has returned to his old lorry driving job, though he no longer smokes 60 cigarettes a day on long journeys. Last year, the Stroke Association reported the case of a London black cab driver who had a stroke, aged 40, who managed to get his cabbies' badge reinstated for a specially adapted vehicle, within 17 months.

Touch wood, I've had few problems driving although I do admit to being inordinately scared whenever I hear someone honking their horn as I am convinced it must be me doing something wrong.

I am also conscious of the amount of planning I do now, even before a fairly short car journey: making sure I know which route I am taking, where I am going to park and whether I have the correct change for the car park. Sometimes, amidst all this planning, I do forget to put petrol in the car, but you can't remember everything.

Going on journeys to anywhere I have not been before requires a planning exercise similar to that prior to the D-Day invasion of Normandy. I use maps, writing out my route on a pad of paper, check internet route planners, even using the multimap (**www.multimap.com**) facility to check aerial photographs of areas or streets I am trying to find. I always make sure, or try and make sure, that I have a mobile phone with me, cash for emergencies and a bottle of mineral water.

So, *physically*, my recovery is probably as complete as I could have hoped for. I still have little feeling in the fingers of my left hand but unless someone was looking specifically at me using that hand, they wouldn't notice it.

Mentally, though, it's far from "business as usual" and there's plenty of room for improvement, though I believe that improvement is happening, albeit gradually, even almost three years on.

For many stroke victims, the "mental" side of stroke boils down to a question of *communication*. This is just one aspect of the *cognitive problems* which accompany stroke, but the loss of speech, or rather the ability to formulate language — to know what you want to say, but be unable to say it — must be the most frustrating.

In my case, my speech was probably the first thing to recover but I know survivors who have recovered much of their "old lives", regaining their independence and even driving again, but not their language. The frustration suffered by survivors who have recovered physically and are mentally "all there" but just cannot express themselves in conventional speech is heartbreaking to see.

In my experience, stroke survivors with speech difficulties are far more likely to suffer from a lack of self-confidence than survivors with a physical disability. I know several who simply prefer isolation at home, not even willing to join survivor groups or one of the excellent dysphasia classes run by the Stroke Association.

Recommended reading

There are two poignant and often harrowing accounts of stroke survivors robbed of the ability to communicate.

Sheila Hale's *The Man Who Lost His Language* (2002) is the moving, sometimes angry, story of the treatment received by her husband the art historian Sir John Hale after his stroke, and subsequent aphasia, in 1992.

Quite remarkable is the story of Jean-Dominique Bauby, the editor of the French Elle magazine, who suffered a massive stroke in his early forties, resulting in the rare condition of "Locked-In Syndrome" which left him completely paralysed, speechless and able only to move one eyelid. With the help of a speech therapist and an "alphabet code", Bauby managed to dictate a memoir, published in English as *The Diving Bell and the Butterfly* (1997). In the title, the Diving Bell refers to the heavy, all encompassing paralysis imposed by the stroke, while the Butterfly is Bauby's mind, still working, fluttering to escape.

I defy anyone to remain unmoved by these books.

These days, no one turns a hair (or should) at the sight of a person in a wheelchair, or with a walking stick, with a walking frame or on one of those electric mobility carts (which have better acceleration than my car). But if someone, however well dressed and however

142

well groomed, who looks physically fit, goes into a shop and then cannot produce a coherent sentence of speech (even though they know exactly what they mean), the automatic reaction is: "They're crazy".

I was not kidding when I suggested to a seminar of stroke nurses and therapists that there ought to be a T-shirt bearing the legend:

> I am not drunk
> I am not mad
> I've had a stroke
> That's all.

Regaining speech

The charity **Speakability** is dedicated to rebuilding communication and issues (among other things) a simple chart describing how to do just that, giving simple, clear advice.

Key points include being patient, being prepared, using props (pen, paper, flashcards, computer screens) and always being positive and encouraging. Above all, never give up.

The other cognitive problems fairly universal among stroke sufferers involve memory and attention.

For me, and I can only speak on behalf of my own battered brain cells, my long term memory seemed to have survived almost intact. I could, for instance, whilst in hospital name 12 novels by John D MacDonald which had colours in the titles, even though I had not read one since 1986. I was inordinately proud of this feat even though the Occupational Therapist, who just wanted to know if I could remember "red" and "blue", seemed less than impressed.

In my first year post-stroke, though, my short term memory was terrible. I would get in the car and forget where I was going. On more than one occasion I forgot where my children's schools were. Best of all were the shopping trips where I would go out for three specific items and come back with five, although none were the three I had gone for. On the worst day, I had to return to the same shop five times.

I would also have trouble with people's names, especially people I met for the first time since the stroke, and if I was in a social situation where there were lots of people around. I soon realised there was no point in trying to be introduced to three people as I would have forgotten the name of the first by the time I got to the third.

This became a problem when trying to find a job after my stroke. It appears that even the lowliest of jobs these days require an interviewing panel of at least three people (particularly in local government) asking what they think are deeply probing, psychologically revealing questions. My problem was not providing the answers, it was that, after about two minutes of each interview, I realised that I hadn't a clue who I was talking to. It must have shown, as I didn't get offered any of the jobs I went for.

Even small and unimportant losses of memory knock the confidence, as does the well meaning fool who says something along the lines of: "When you get to our age . . ."

In an attempt to snap myself out of this, I began to make notes of "Things To Do" and the family helped by setting up a whiteboard and marker memo board in the kitchen for routine chores, as well as a write on calendar. I would also make detailed shopping lists and, naturally, I would then forget to take them with me when I went shopping.

Yet I am convinced that this sort of self-discipline did help, as my short term memory has certainly improved in the past year. I still write notes to myself, but now, more often than not, I remember where I put them.

Poor short term memory

Some survivors use their PCs as a diary and reminder board, which is fine as long as you remember to look at your computer every day. I am, by nature, a scribbler in ink on paper, and so I find jotting down a key word or two on even the scrappiest bit of paper works for me.

As a matter of routine now, I try to plan for each morning the night before, even if all I am doing is taking the kids to school. If I am doing anything else, I try to have everything pre-prepared, ready for me to collect as I lead the post-breakfast exodus from the house.

In most instances, the system works, though any interruption to or deviation from the routine, however small, will throw me completely. I know I am bad at keeping an appointments diary. For over 20 years working in the brewing industry in London, I lived by my office appointments diary and, before that, my life as a journalist would be ruled by the newspaper's diary.

These days, when I could really use one, I almost invariably forget to consult it. (Much to the disgust of my younger daughter who now buys me one each Christmas.) I will be offered a hospital appointment for the following month, say, and agree to it immediately. Only when I get home (if I remember to check) do I realise that is *the one day* that month that I have to be somewhere else, doing something I've known about for six months. Very humbly, I have to ring up and change the appointment. Actually, it has happened to me so often that now it would feel rather strange to be given an appointment and have me stick to it. What I should do, of course, is not accept anything on the spot, or remember to take my diary with me for once.

Most stroke survivors suffer what are usually known as attention problems, although I tend to think of them as problems of keeping concentration.

It affects different people in different ways, of course, but most commonly, stroke survivors can find themselves easily distracted or unable to concentrate on a person speaking to them, or unable to concentrate on more than one thing at once or to exclude distracting background information, such as traffic noise or piped music.

The result of any or all of these symptoms is invariably frustration leading to outbursts of temper, impulsiveness, memory loss and exhaustion.

In my own case, I think I have identified three specific areas where, mentally, I simply don't function like I used to. If my brain was the engine of a car, you could probably say it was 30% less efficient these days — at least that is what it feels like most days.

One of the nicest things said to me since the stroke, was by theatre director Adrian Stokes, whom I ran into on the street, about 18 months after coming out of hospital. We had not seen each other for about three years and so I told him about the stroke and, naturally, he asked how I felt now, as physically I looked in fair shape.

"I reckon I'm about 30% slower mentally," I said.

"Well, that'll give the rest of us a chance, then," he quipped.

The first of these concentration or "attention" problems manifested itself in what an actor on stage would call "drying" — when they forget a line and "dry" in front of an audience. I have no idea if this is a direct result of the stroke or a side effect of the medications I have taken, as it did not begin until several months after the stroke.

I first noticed it whilst answering the phone. It was just an ordinary phone call, though I can't now remember who had rung, and a social one — absolutely nothing stressful or dramatic — yet after a couple of minutes I suddenly found myself going hoarse and feeling very thirsty. Within seconds, or so it seemed, my throat tightened and then I simply could not speak at all. I must have made some sort of mumbling apology and hung up, leaving a very confused person on the other end of the line.

This began to happen with frustrating regularity to the extent that I became totally paranoid about the telephone. I never called anyone and only answered a ringing phone if absolutely necessary when there was no one else in the house. For four months, I never turned my mobile phone on, relying entirely on email for day to day communication with the outside world.

Where once I had regularly appeared on local radio either as a "spokesman for the brewing industry" or talking about crime fiction, the thought of even recording a piece, let alone going on live, absolutely terrified me.

No one could come up with an explanation for this condition beyond the fact, as one nurse said, I was having "a stroke moment". I saw a Speech Therapist who ran me through a series of breathing and speaking exercises and could not find anything obviously wrong with me — although the fact that I "dried up" on her in the middle of the tests did convince her there was some sort of problem.

I was referred to an Ear Nose and Throat specialist who poked an optical camera up my nose and down my throat (one of the most unpleasant things that has ever happened to me) and he too could find nothing physically wrong, although he did advise me to sip a drink whilst talking. I perked up immediately at this advice, until I realised he meant water.

Talking on the phone

My Ear Nose and Throat doctor was an Indian, who had studied medicine at Edinburgh University. He not only advised me to have water on hand if I was making a phone call, but gave me the tip that lukewarm water would be better than iced water from the fridge, which would have been my natural choice.

It was, he said, a trick he had learned as a medical student in curry eating competitions with Malaysian students. The Malays always insisted on warm water to drink with the hottest curries, leaving the "amateurs" who had opted for ice cold lager way behind.

As I slowly learned to control my blood pressure, the condition seemed to fade away. Perhaps it was always psychological and simply believing that if I kept sipping water I wouldn't dry was enough to make sure I didn't. Whatever the cause and however I cured it, it is a nice twist of fate that nowadays I reach for a glass of water when the phone rings whereas once I would have automatically grabbed for my cigarettes and lighter.

The fear of drying (and therefore looking an idiot in public) kept me well away from speaking in public for several months, but in July 2003 I was called upon to present the annual *Sherlock* Awards, on behalf of the

Sherlock Detective Magazine, at the Crime Scene convention being held at the National Film Theatre on London's Southbank. It was a difficult thing to get out of as I had been involved in the awards from their inception (given to crime writers for novels and also TV detectives). I had even won an honorary *Sherlock* myself, and so felt duty-bound.

I agreed to do it with some trepidation, but only if I could co-present with my old mate Colin (Inspector Morse) Dexter and only if I could write a script for the event, which both of us would rigidly stick to.

The event went well, or at least without any embarrassing incidents, partly because I had a bottle of mineral water with me at all times and partly because I just knew Colin couldn't stick to a pre-prepared script if you held a gun to his head, so I was prepared for his ad-libbing and didn't let it throw me into a panic.

A year on from that, I was asked to present a spoof quiz show "I'm Sorry I Haven't A Cluedo" at the Harrogate Festival. It was a format I had developed for a crime writers' convention in 1999 and involved two teams of very competitive crime writers answering silly questions for laughs rather than points. To help me present this, I had as my faithful sidekicks two crime writers who are also professional actors: Stella Duffy and Martyn Waites. I insisted on scripting the whole (live) show, right down to the last ad-lib and briefed Stella and Martyn that I might well dry and, if I did, they had to be able to take on my part as well.

150

I was genuinely scared that I would collapse under the pressure and I managed to convince them I was.

Fortunately, it seemed to go smoothly enough and when, two minutes before our alloted time ran out, Stella showed her script to the audience and said, "Bloody hell, there's another nine pages of this!", I knew I had survived.

The second attention problem I experienced was far more dramatic in many ways and certainly more distressing for me. For want of a better description, I have come to call this syndrome or condition or side effect (whatever it is) my *interruptions*.

Quite simply, if I am speaking and am interrupted by something totally unexpected, I completely lose my train of thought and I do mean completely, sometimes to the extent that I suddenly don't know *who* I'm supposed to be talking to, let alone what I was saying or what we were even talking about. With drying it was a question of knowing what to say, but not being able to get the words out because my voice box had gone on strike. With the interruptions it is almost like instant amnesia. I can speak perfectly well, but don't know what to say. Most times, which is really frightening, *I don't even know if it is my turn to speak.*

If the drying leaves me gasping and gagging like a drowning man struggling for air, then the interruptions leave me blank faced and dead eyed, probably looking like a sheep with a mild headache.

It can be sparked off in a number of ways, especially when someone does interrupt me mid-sentence. Although not always. I like to think I am still capable of a normal social conversation, or a well reasoned, civilised debate or even argument about books, sport, politics, music — the normal things you talk about. But if someone jumps in with a remark that I find unexpected or says exactly what I was just planning to say, then my concentration goes and my thought processes come to a shuddering halt.

The worst example of all is when someone, trying to be funny (and I have done this myself in the past), deliberately misunderstands what I am saying and starts asking "stupid" questions which under normal circumstances would probably lead to quite amusing repartee. That sort of distraction does exactly that; it distracts me totally. If I think I am trying to say something important and I know that my train of thought has now been derailed, I cannot stop myself getting angry.

It can happen in other ways. In a hotel bar quite recently, a wall mounted television was blasting out non-stop MTV coverage. At first, as the bar was quite crowded, I almost didn't notice the sound over the background hubbub but, after about 10 minutes, a group of about 20 hotel residents stood up *en masse* to go into the restaurant. With suddenly fewer people in the bar, the noise from the MTV channel seemed to go up a notch to exactly the right level (almost the same frequency it seemed) to interrupt whatever I was trying to say to the group I was with. Despite several requests, the bar staff were unable to turn down the volume which was centrally controlled by some hotel computer and we had to move into the lobby area, by which time, of course, I had totally forgotten what I had been trying to say.

On another occasion I was talking to a friend I had known for years. It was a hot summer's day and he was about to get into his car to leave. We were chatting away quite happily until he reached into his car to turn on the engine to run the air conditioning to cool it down before his long journey home. The gentle throb of the car's engine ticking over (it was only a Volvo, after all) sounded to me like a pneumatic drill inside my head and any attempt at continuing a conversation was useless. Embarrassed, unable to explain and with no memory at all of what I had been saying a few seconds before, I turned on my heel and stomped back into our house leaving my wife to say goodbye and to gloss over my erratic behaviour. When she asked me what I thought I was doing, in the way that wives do, all I could offer by way of explanation was a rather limp: "I just couldn't compete with that engine."

Numbers can be just as bad, if not worse, than words. I discovered this whilst running the annual second hand book stall at the village fayre. At busy times with lots of customers and children milling around the stall, I found that even the slightest distraction whilst I was serving someone meant that I went totally blank when it came to giving the correct change. This was despite what I had thought was a foolproof scheme of pricing all the books at either 20p or 10p before we started, to make life easy.

My third attention problem is what I learned was known as Emotional Lability. The best way to describe the feeling is to use a good old fashioned expression: you "fill up" with emotion.

It can be triggered by extreme joy or by extreme sadness and results in an almost immediate welling-up of tears and chest bursting sobs which rack the body and make the lips quiver uncontrollably. Alternatively, usually when it is most inappropriate, it manifests itself as hysterical giggles.

Of all the strange behaviour I have exhibited since the stroke, from walking into door frames to bouts of black depression, I think it is these unexpected bursts of sobbing which still bemuse and upset my younger children. It is quite difficult to explain to an 11-year-old why Daddy is apparently crying during the Last Night of the Proms when everyone on the television seems to be having such a happy time. Ironically, a sense of extreme pride in something my children have achieved or said is one of the things which sets me off.

There are some things I just know will open the floodgates, from tragic pictures of starvation in Africa during Live8 to any film where characters have to be brave and stiff upper lipped in the face of terrible odds (virtually anything with John Mills in it).

I can't see what I can do about this particular legacy of the stroke. It is not painful and it does not really affect my quality of life even if it is incredibly embarrassing at times. The saddest aspect of it is that I might never be able to watch *Casablanca* again.

CHAPTER
NINE

Diagnosis

Have I learned anything from my stroke?

I have certainly learned a lot *about* strokes, but then I knew virtually nothing before. The sum total of my knowledge was that strokes happened to old people, not people of my age with a mortgage to pay and kids still at school, and were often fatal or led to permanent disabilities.

Working for Different Strokes I have come across cases of stroke happening to toddlers barely a year old and the brave mother of a daughter who had a stroke aged 16, but 10 years on was taking her legal exams to qualify as a solicitor.

So that's one important lesson: strokes can happen to anyone at any age. The other obvious one is that recovery is possible — not in every case and sometimes only partially, and there are still yawning gaps in the provision of rehabilitation facilities and services in this country. Far too many stroke survivors leave hospital and simply disappear off the map.

Stroke is by its nature an isolating disease. In the first instance it isolates you as a person from your brain, then from parts of your body, your memory, your ability to communicate, your capacity to understand what is happening. The effect of this is to isolate you from your family and loved ones, your work, your social life, your life outside your home or a hospital ward.

It is the cruellest and loneliest of afflictions.

I have learned a lot about blood pressure and hypertension, that "silent" disease which gives you no warning or telltale symptoms.

With stroke itself, I empowered myself by finding out as much as I could about it, on the basis of Know Thine Enemy.

The same is true about blood pressure. Knowing what I know now, and bearing in mind that my mother suffered from high blood pressure and I probably inherited it from her, I would like to have thought I would have been more aware in middle age of the need for giving up smoking, weight loss, cutting out salt and taking more exercise. All the boring things you promise yourself you will get round to doing one day.

Would they have prevented the stroke? Who knows? I do them now to prevent having another one. That is too terrifying a prospect to ignore.

As the detective hero of my books would say: "It's better to be lucky than good", but no one can rely on being that lucky twice.